MO

–

A Route to Intelligence?

Bob Cory

Published by: Parklands Press

Published by: Parklands Press
ISBN: 978-0-9928102-0-7
Printed January 2014
First Edition – this is the paper edition
first published for Kindle in October 2013

Reprinted March 2015

Website: www.mopeks.org

MOPEKS®

This book is the companion to the computer program MOPEKS which is available here: www.mopeks.org. You can access it from your Kindle or other mobile device but it will be much easier to use a laptop or desktop computer.

You can download the latest fully functioning version of MOPEKS without any kind of charge, registration or tricks. You do not need a credit card. Just click on the link, install it and run it for as long as you like. It is “freeware” in the real sense of the word. It is not an attempt to make money, it is an attempt to demonstrate what I believe to be a new approach to Artificial Intelligence.

This book is a record of the journey that gave rise to MOPEKS and sets out a possible route to actually building a Silicon Based Intelligent Entity (‘SBIE’).

Table of Contents

Introduction

"Trying is the first step towards failure" Homer Simpson

It is normal when developing something to extensively research the literature and immerse oneself in the field. The problem with this is that there are some 100,000 papers published every year on the subject of artificial intelligence and the human brain. To even have a cursory glance at a field of literature this large is going to be difficult.

The other aspect of this is that it seems to me that for 70 years the field of artificial intelligence has been stalled. In the middle of the twentieth century people felt it would be fairly simple to produce a computer program that had genuine intelligence but I see little evidence of such programs emerging. This is one of these things which is always going to be with us in 20 years' time – like nuclear fusion.

Accordingly, it seemed to me that I might as well just start in a vacuum exploring my own ideas. The chances of these being successful was obviously small but MOPEKS and this book are the outcome and you can judge it on its own merits.

Certain aspects of MOPEKS are the subject of patent applications in all of the major countries in the world. The name MOPEKS is a registered trademark and the logo displayed on the front cover is also a trademark. To quote the Wright brothers "we did not do this to make money but if anybody is going to make money, it should be us."

Chapter 1

Is it Possible to build a SBIE?

"Every mountain top is within reach if you just keep climbing"
Barry Finlay, Kilimanjaro and Beyond

The task is to build a Silicon Based Intelligent Entity. A SBIE for short. I have deliberately used the somewhat pompous phrase "Intelligent Entity" rather than Computer or Computer Program because it is possible that it would need some combination of the two that is neither a recognisable computer nor software.

Is it Achievable in Principle?

Before we go any further, let's try and save ourselves some time by considering whether it is achievable in principle. Or, whether, like a Perpetual Motion Machine, it is literally impossible because of the fundamental laws of physics and not worth wasting time on.

Well, the fact that we exist and are intelligent is enough to satisfy **me** that it is theoretically possible – we are meat computers. Not everybody who disagrees with me is stupid, so let's examine this a little more closely.

The objectors seem to fall into two main camps – those who say that there is something essentially spiritual and God given about the human brain and those who concede that there is nothing magical about it but that it depends on obscure or unknown science.

Let's take the religious objections first. For hundreds of years people of a religious disposition have fought a rearguard action against scientific progress. They believe that we are somehow "special" rather than just the result of blind evolutionary forces. In the past they argued that the sun went round the earth, that organic materials were not just ordinary chemicals and that the world was created 5,000 years ago.

Many religions believe that human beings have souls which distinguish us from animals and some of their supporters feel that to create an artificially intelligent entity would somehow violate that distinction. Well, maybe it would but I have never yet heard of a scientific experiment which has produced an unexpected result which can only be explained by a creator. Indeed, one of the wonders of the universe is **The Unreasonable Effectiveness of Mathematics in the Natural Sciences**, to quote a paper by the physicist Eugene Wigner. There are no real mysteries – just problems that have not yet been solved.

So, until God starts interfering, let's just carry on. Incidentally, a good example of profound interference is given in Carl Sagan's novel **Contact** in which it is found that after a few million places of decimals, the digits of pi actually display a perfect circle when regarded as parameters in a graphical display. To pull off a trick like that you would need to be able not only to create a universe but also specify its laws to millions of decimal places. That would certainly show the presence of a creator. And one with a sense of humour too. Something sorely lacking in all religions – apart from Pastafarianism, of course.

In fact, if you can do that I will certainly give you respec' and a capital "C" as in "Creator." I might even praise You, if that's what You really want. Certainly if you take the Bible as a guide He is really desperate for praise. To me, this is pretty pathetic. Why on earth would a divine creator want praise from the creatures he has created? Would you like a flock of sheep which spent all day bleating about how wonderful you were? We are talking divinity here, not Justin Bieber. It shows an astonishing lack of self confidence, in my opinion.

As for the objection that human intelligence relies on unknown science, I cannot help feeling that religious belief is somehow lurking in the background or maybe just pure ego – "I am special, even if you aren't." On what conceivable grounds can you suppose that something you find difficult to explain is impossible because of unknown science?

Even if unknown science **is** involved, that would not necessarily mean that the task is impossible, as I hope to show right now.

Do we need to understand everything involved?

The next question which presents itself is whether it is possible to create a SBIE without really understanding the underlying science and engineering? It is tempting to react immediately by saying that it is impossible – how can you build something if you don't understand how it works? Obviously, people who are responsible for the creation of aircraft understand the principles of aerodynamics and if they did not, their planes would fall out of the sky. Similarly, engine creators understand how engines work and computer chips are created by people who have a considerable grasp of electronic computing.

A little more thought will show that this argument is spurious. We are surrounded by enormously complex machines which were built without the slightest insight into how they work. And yet they function superbly well. I refer of course, to living creatures created by the blind forces of evolution (explored in the next chapter). There is no intelligence or insight behind evolution. The mechanism works like this:

Step 1. Allow trillions of random molecules covering millions of square miles of surface to interact under the influence of sunlight, wind, atmospheric gases, temperature variation and particle bombardment until totally by accident you arrive at a molecule (probably quite a long one – there is a theoretical minimum length, I believe) which can produce copies of itself.

Step 2. Wait for a few billion years.

That is all you have to do. Maybe one day we will arrive at a lifeless planet and observe the process up close. But even one hundred years is a long time, never mind billions – so, how can we speed this up a bit?

Well, we can go to the other extreme and instruct an experienced and intelligent human being to design a machine to our specification and build it. If he knows what he is doing and has a 3-D printer the machine may be ready and working in a few days.

Or how about a compromise? Let's take James Dyson, the English inventor of the cyclonic vacuum cleaner. By his own admission, when he started he knew nothing about the science of airflow – he just built something and when it didn't work, modified it and tried again. Eventually he arrived at something that did work. Last year his company made £300M pre-tax profits – not bad for somebody who doesn't know what he is doing. Let's try and summarise this process, which is usually known as "trial and error".

Step 1: Design and build something which you feel may do the job

Step 2: Try it out

Step 3: If you can see and understand why it does not work, re-design it and build a new prototype and return to Step 2. If you cannot see why it does not work, randomly change some aspect of the design and return to Step 2.

In James Dyson's case, this process took five years and involved hundreds of prototypes (he has claimed there were 5,000 prototypes but that cannot be true – do the maths). What is true is that the result took a major share of the market and humiliated the major companies in his field.

Before we conclude, let's look at a couple of useful engineering concepts – ducks and black boxes.

Ducks

"If it looks like a duck, swims like a duck, and quacks like a duck, then it's a duck."

In other words, there are circumstances where the internal nature and mechanics of a machine or a process are irrelevant.

What matters is how it interacts with the outside world. It is well known that the American Condor (Cathartidae) evolved independently from the African Vulture (Accipitridae). These are fundamentally different creatures with different DNA but they both look and act like vultures. So they are vultures. If you are dying in the desert and see them circling overhead, there is little point in working out whether they are Cathartidae or Accipitridae. They will do what vultures do.

An example from economics. A man may take enormous pride in creating cakes which are as good as he can make them irrespective of cost. His customers greatly appreciate his efforts and a queue forms each morning outside his shop waiting for it to open. The products sell like hot cakes (not surprising when you think about it) and he makes a good living. But profit is not his driving motivation.

[If you live in Milborne Port, Somerset, you will realise I am talking about my uncle David Coombs, who sadly died some years ago.]

Somebody else, whose motivation is purely to make money, may also have concluded (maybe by looking at Apple) that the way to make a fortune is to build a fantastic and beautiful product or service for which people will pay a very high price. Accordingly, he devotes every waking moment to making his customers extremely happy.

The DNA, or driving force, of these two organisations is different but the outcome is the same. Happy customers and well rewarded shareholders.

Black Boxes

Another related concept is that of the "black box." We have no idea what is inside the black box or how it works but it has a wire labelled "input" and another wire labelled "output." Fortunately, we have a large number of these black boxes with the same serial number on them so we can test them to destruction if we need to. After extensive tests, we discover that the output is a sine wave whose frequency varies in direct proportion to the incoming voltage. And at over 20 volts it melts. That is all we need to know in order to use it.

To add a note of caution here, some black boxes may be trickier than that. It would not be difficult to design a black box that would give a totally different set of responses once a year on 1st April. But generally, the concept of the black box works.

Black boxes are extremely common in electronics. If you are designing an electronic device you may well need a chip to turn 5 volts into 20 volts. All you do is look in a catalogue and find a device that does just that at the right price, size, current and efficiency. Then you literally plug it in and solder up the connections. How it works is a mystery but it does work and that is all that matters.

A more interesting kind of black box is the Square Root of Minus One, or "i", as it is usually written. At school you were told that a negative number cannot have a square root, so how can "i" exist? Well, it probably doesn't exist but that doesn't stop you from using it. All you need to know is that:

$$i \times i = -1$$

If you are an electrical engineer you can then use "i" to do all sorts of interesting and useful things. So this is an example of using something that we don't understand, and indeed does not even exist to do something useful.

Is it Achievable in Practice?

Just because something can be done in principle does not mean that you can actually do it. It is quite possible in principle to throw a hundred sixes one after the other when throwing dice but hell will freeze over first. So, maybe it can be done but is effectively impossible? Maybe because evolution has access to resources (eg a hundred billion tons of bacteria) that we are unable to use.

Of all the reasons why it may be impossible to build a SBIE, this seems to me to be the most likely.

But let's just try anyway.

Chapter 2

Evolution

"Building a better mousetrap merely results in smarter mice"
Charles Darwin

Before we start trying to build a SBIE, let's look at the most potent weapon in nature's armoury.

Evolution is an immensely powerful force and is responsible for the creation of life on earth. It may even, in the context of multiple universes, be responsible for the fact that our universe is uniquely fitted for the evolution of life. But that is another story.

Survival of the Fattest

Ask the average person what evolution means to them and they will reply "I don't believe in evolution" or "it's the survival of the fittest ... or something." Fitness does seem a desirable quality and many of us have feelings of guilt when we slump in front of the TV eating popcorn and twinges of equally guilty pleasure when we read of some unfortunate fitness fanatic who has died of a heart attack at the age of 40.

So how about "survival of the fattest" as a mantra? The idea that gorging to your hearts content could increase your chances of survival would certainly have consumer appeal. So let's look at the evidence. Life has been around for about four billion years if the latest geological evidence is correct. Supermarkets and Social Security, on the other hand, have only been around for about seventy years in the UK. In many parts of the world fatness (as opposed to fitness) is still seen as a very desirable quality and for a very good reason. If your food supply is sporadic and uncertain then the ability to turn food into reserves of fat may well make the difference between survival and death.

Incidentally, not everybody has this ability – I once knew a very pretty and very skinny girl who would have two starters and two main courses when she went out to dinner. Yes, really – not every skinny girl is on a diet.

Obesity is not a disease – it is an evolutionary feature designed to increase your chances of survival in certain circumstances. I am tall and skinny in case you think I am arguing to justify being fat. When I was young I even had a six-pack (now replaced by a barrel)

If you were trapped in a bijou basement apartment in Notting Hill with a huge supply of sparkling mineral water and rocket leaf salad how long could you last? Well, if you are built like the average western adult the chances are that you could survive for several weeks and emerge feeling very weak and a couple of stone lighter but fundamentally in good health.

Unless you were a supermodel. In which case after a couple of days your body's need for energy would be such that it would start to consume your muscles and soon your brain as well ("like wow, that didn't take very long") and very shortly you would be dead. As Mariah Carey was portrayed as saying in a skit "whenever I watch TV and I see those poor starving kids all over the world, I can't help but cry. I mean I would love to be skinny like that, but not with all those flies and death and stuff."

Yes, in many parts of the world flies and death and stuff are still very much around.

When we say that evolution is the survival of the fittest (as opposed to the fattest), we mean that living organisms which are most suited to the circumstances in which they find themselves will prosper. Stated like this it sounds like a cliché but like many things which sound obvious it was far from obvious when it was first stated and even now is not accepted by many people of a religious persuasion. This is not because they really think evolution is false, it is rather because somebody else has told them what to think. As Will Rogers said, “faith is believing what you know is not true.”

There is no value judgment involved in the term fitness. Under some circumstances being very fat may help and in others being able to run 100 meters very fast may be more useful. Fitness extends to other qualities such as mental attributes. For instance, always telling the truth may help you prosper in a small community but in politics the ability to lie convincingly is far more useful.

How can you tell when politicians are lying? Their mouths open.

Reproduction

“Had God consulted me in the matter, I should have advised him to continue the generation of the species by fashioning them out of clay” Martin Luther

“Survival of the fittest” is not the whole story. Survival is a good start but it is not enough – you have to pass on your genetic material to others. As far as animals are concerned, that means having children who in turn survive and pass on their genetic material to their offspring and so on. It is this necessity that is responsible for many of the more regrettable tendencies of human beings. Especially the males. A man who goes round impregnating dozens of women (whether by charm, lies or violence) has a much higher chance of perpetuating his genetic material than a man who is faithful to one person and has 2.3 children. Ghengis Khan is said to have millions of descendants – he didn't do that by staying at home with the wife. Or maybe he did it by staying at home with the wives. "Thousands of 'em", to quote Michael Caine from a different context.

Female animals have a different perspective. The key difference between male and female animals is that a male can have hundreds of children in a year but a female cannot have more than a few. So, a man can maximise the chances of his genetic material surviving by having sex with any female who can be persuaded or bullied into it. A woman maximises the chances of her genetic material surviving by having sex only with men who can provide good genetic material and an environment in which children can prosper.

Nearly all of the problems between men and women can be explained by this critical distinction. As you queue up at the supermarket checkout, the headlines will scream out at you. "He slept with my best friend – how could he betray me like that?" "Tiger Woods slept with dozens of Women." "Bill Clinton and the Intern." And so it goes on. Why does a famous and successful man put everything at risk to have sex with the cleaner? Are you there Arnold Schwarzenegger and Dominic Strauss Kahn, almost President of France? Well folks, they are not sex addicts or power mad. They are just normal human males with a bias towards action who have been programmed by evolution to maximise the chances of the survival of their genetic material. By screwing everything in sight.

When the farmer lets the ram into a field of sheep, does it find one sheep and form a faithful and loving relationship? 'Fraid not. It systematically mates with every single sheep – once. They know that because the ram has a coloured dye marker strapped to his belly – are you listening, Hillary? When you see a field of sheep, each with a single red mark on its back, you will know what has been going on. If you ever see a field of sheep where just one of them has its back absolutely covered in dye and all the other sheep are still virgins, please take a film and put it on Youtube because this is a unique event – never seen before in the history of the world. Don't blame me – blame evolution. Or maybe blame God, if you believe in Intelligent Design (or is Satan in charge of that department?)

Sexual Selection

As suggested above, another aspect of evolution is Sexual Selection. The mechanism that gives rise to the peacock's tail and super-cool guys like Marlon Brando and Jimi Hendrix. Or super-hot chicks like Angelina Jolie and Kelly Brooks. The kind of people you spot across a crowded room and feel your heart go all a'flutter. Being sexually irresistible gives a big advantage when it comes to either persuading a woman to let you breed with her or persuading a man to look after your children. So, in the case of human beings, we could rephrase evolution as "the survival of the best adapted breeding stock." It doesn't exactly trip off the tongue, but there you are.

Genes

Are we there yet? Not quite, there is a little bit more to consider. So far, we have only considered the mechanism whereby organisms which are adapted to their environments and sexually successful will tend to survive and produce successful offspring whereas those that are not, do not.

We take it for granted that the genetic material passed on is essentially the same as that of the parents and ancestors of the two parties involved but maybe mashed up a bit? “He’s got your eyes but his father’s chin.” This mechanism works by each party contributing genes to the mix. Genes are the chunks of DNA that determine all of your characteristics – if you have big feet and green eyes that is the fault of your genes. Popular culture leads us to believe that there is a gene for everything but the reality can be more complex. High intelligence, for example, stems from a large number of genes none of which contribute more than a tiny bit to your intelligence but together they do the job. On the other hand, eye colour comes from a single gene.

Everybody has two copies of each gene and genes come in dominant and recessive flavours. This is beginning to look complicated but like many apparently complicated things, once you understand it, it is pretty simple. If somebody cannot explain something then the chances are that they do not really understand it! So, let’s take an example. Suppose both your mother and father have brown hair but they actually each have a brown gene and a blond gene. You inherit a random gene from each of them so there is only a 25% chance that you will inherit two blond genes. If you do then you will have blond hair. On the other hand, if you have a blond gene and a brown gene, the brown gene dominates and you will have brown hair. That is why genuine blonds are pretty rare in the UK.

If you are a purist, substitute the word "allele" for "gene" above.

So, we all resemble our ancestors – I am grumpy like my grandfather and useless at remembering things, like my mother. There is no doubt that even if genetic material always stayed the same in principle there would be an element of evolution in the sense that the survivors become more successful. But even the best sheep will still be sheep. So how does a sheep turn into a tiger?

New Species

As discussed above every single aspect of our physical makeup is dictated by our genetic material. So how does a sheep turn into a tiger? A better question would be, how does something like the human eye come about? Surely it is far too complex to have resulted from chance? Let's answer that with another question. How can you climb a mountain 27,000 feet high (about 8,000 metres) when the highest step you can make is only about a foot or so?

We all know the answer to that – you do it one step at a time. And that is how evolution works – one step at a time. A series of tiny changes can bring about an organism that is very different from its ancestors. The actual mechanism is that the organism concerned experiences changes in its genes. There are at least four ways this can happen.

1. Its existing operational genes change by random copying errors – "Mutation"

2. Its existing operational genes change by random impact from radiation eg from cosmic rays – “Mutation”, again
3. It borrows genes from elsewhere – “Horizontal Gene Transfer”
4. “Orphan Genes” come out of nowhere ...

Mutation means that the coding of the gene – made up of DNA, is altered. A molecule of DNA is knocked out of position or a whole chunk is moved from one place to another. Most of the time this means that the gene will stop working but occasionally it will result in an improvement. So, to take an extreme example, at some point in history an animal was born with two stomachs as the result of an accident in the gene factory. Normally, it would have died but in this case it was uniquely able to digest grass and this gave it a huge advantage. Its children survived whereas the children of single stomached animals starved to death. Within a few thousand years the double stomached animals dominated the landscape.

Please note that as with the cow with two stomachs, a tiny change in the DNA does not necessarily bring about a tiny change in the structure of the creature concerned. Somewhere in our DNA is an instruction like this: “number of arms = 2.” An unfortunate encounter with a high energy particle could change that so that you are born with four arms.

Horizontal Gene Transfer can take place when the body absorbs a virus or bacteria and gains access to some of its genetic material. For example, some water borne bacteria glow in the dark. If you can somehow assimilate such bacteria into your genetic makeup then maybe you can also glow in the dark? That may get you eaten or maybe it will attract a mate? In the latter case you have gained an advantage and soon the lake will be full of your glowing descendants. Or not.

Orphan Genes are genes which suddenly come out of nowhere. They do not seem to have parents. Until recently this was thought to be a very rare occurrence because genes are very complicated so how can they come from nowhere? Well, it turns out, they probably come from changes in junk DNA which makes up about 97% of the human body. Really, it is better to consider this not as junk but as a reservoir of potential genes. A store room full of old broken machines and spare parts – pop into any home workshop. But out of which something operational may emerge with a few dexterous changes. It is possible that I was one of the first people to realise this.

Evolution's fuel

› 22 April 2000 by **Bob Cory**
› Magazine issue 2235.

Your article speculates on the role of "junk" DNA (1 April, p 38). My experience with self-evolving computer programs is that they evolve much more quickly and successfully if they have plenty of "junk" instructions to help them mutate. Conversely, structures in which every component is critical typically collapse when something changes randomly.

If this applies equally in biology, one would expect to find the fastest-evolving creatures to be those with the highest percentage of junk DNA. Since human beings have evolved quicker (or further, anyway) than any other living entity, it is not surprising to find we score 97 per cent on the junk index.

It would be fascinating to see how coelacanths and other "living fossils"which have failed to evolverate in comparison.

Figure 2.01 New Scientist

Back to the evolution of the eye. As is well documented elsewhere, the eye has actually evolved many times quite independently. It starts off with a patch of skin that is slightly sensitive to light because of some changed or acquired gene. That enables the creature to maybe move away or towards the light to obtain food. It also enables it to gain an awareness that there is something near it blocking out or altering the light. Something that it can eat or avoid. This gives it a huge advantage and pretty soon the lake is full of creatures that can sense light. Then one of its descendants is born with a saucer shaped depression of the light sensitive area of skin. This means that it cannot just sense the light but work out where it is coming from.

The next step is a flap of very thin transparent skin over the area concerned which keeps out water and other invaders. Then the thickness of the skin flap varies and suddenly the eye has a lens. And so it goes on with an endless number of small improvements. One major problem with evolution as discussed later is that each step must be an improvement – it really struggles to climb a mountain with a moat round it.

Epigenetics

This is tricky so please concentrate. Under different conditions, the instructions in your DNA may turn on or off stretches of genes resulting in a different physical organism but with no change in the underlying genetic structure. To take an example, suppose a pair of identical twins are born but separated at birth (this used to be very common). One goes to a very hot country and the other goes to a very cold country. Twenty years later we find that the one in the cold country is short and fat and the one in the hot country is tall and skinny. But they both have identical DNA so how did that happen? Well, they each have a sensor that detects average temperature and turns off appropriate genes. So, in the cold country the fat genes are turbocharged and the height genes are dampened down. In the hot country the reverse happens. This is obviously a made up example but hopefully the message is clear.

Computer programmers will recognise Epigenetics as the direct equivalent of a Preprocessor Directive. So, if your program is running on a PC under Windows 98 (an ancient operating system) it will cut out sections of code that will not work on such a set up. If on the other hand, your PC is running Windows 8 (the very latest operating system) it will incorporate all of your latest and most sophisticated code.

At some point Microsoft will bring out Windows -82. *[The series "98", "8", "-82". Subtract 90 each time? No? Well, I thought it was moderately funny but you're probably right.]*

Punctuated Equilibrium

As outlined above, evolution can only proceed one step at a time but even a tiny, tiny advantage will put you ahead of the game over millions of years. A casino has maybe a 1% to 5% advantage over you but will wipe you out in an evening – where do you think the £100,000 per week running costs come from? Certainly not from all those people who are "just about breaking even." Even a 0.0000000000000000001% advantage will tell if there are trillions of other bacteria just like you and we can wait for millions of years if necessary.

Having said that, in my experience of computerised evolution, the population change comes very quickly indeed. Long periods where nothing seems to be happening and then suddenly the new species emerges with a bang. In the world of biologists and archeologists this is known as Punctuated Equilibrium and is regarded as something of a mystery.

It seems to me that it is likely that this happens because the process of evolution has reached a point where it is necessary to make a big leap forward (to quote Chairman Mao) in order to jump over the moat surrounding the mountain, as mentioned previously.

This may well require two or more changes to take place simultaneously – not just one mutation or gene transfer but several. So if the odds of each is one in a million, the odds of three changes happening simultaneously is one in a million million million. Hence the long wait. It is like being held up by a road accident – once you get past the bottleneck you can continue to make progress.

That explains the long delay but what about the big burst of progress when you get past the bottleneck – evolution normally only takes small steps? Well, it may be that it has entered a channel where success is inevitable.

Imagine a giant game show where you are in a room which has a thousand exits. Only one of these lead to the outside world and the rest are immediate dead ends. This means that you need, on average, to try about 500 doors before you hit the right one. When you find that door you score 10 points.

But the route from the real exit door has 5 forks in the road before it reaches the outside world so you then have 32 possible routes to explore. When you finally get out you score

100 points. This means that as soon as you score 10 points you are only 16 tries (on average) from success. So, the spectators, as soon as they see the 10 points come up start cheering because they know that you will emerge very shortly with 100 points. So, a long delay while you find the correct door but once you find it, progress is very quick.

Or consider Mount Snowdon which at 3,560 ft (1,085 m), is the highest mountain in Wales. Yes, I know that is pathetic on a world scale but bear with me. As it happens there is a handy path that runs all the way up to the top. Once you have found the path, it is simple to walk up it. But finding it will take you all week – even longer than waiting for service in a UK restaurant. Punctuated equilibrium.

Recent Evolution

We tend to assume that evolution takes place over a time-scale measured in millions or hundreds of millions of years and as far as the evolution of new species or devices (eg the eye) is concerned, it does. But it also takes place all around us on a surprisingly short time frame. When the motor car was invented the roads were covered with dead birds – hundreds per mile and people were seriously concerned that the entire bird population would be wiped out. Bear in mind that this slaughter was inflicted by just a few thousand cars, not the millions that are on the road today. So what happened? Did the birds learn about cars or get smarter or tell each other “don’t land on the road, look what happened to our Billie?” Well, some of the smarter ones, such as rooks (see Chapter 6) probably **did** tell each other but evolution also played its part.

Birds who liked feeding on roads died quickly but nervous birds who didn't, lived to breed. The same will happen with wind turbines – birds with a propensity to fly through them will breed less (because they are dead). So, the genetic propensity to avoid turbines will spread throughout the bird population. Not that I like wind turbines particularly – silly things built by politicians trying to get the eco vote. Salvation will come via hundreds of square miles of desert covered in very inefficient (but very cheap) solar panels.

[The solar panels will also cool down the areas they cover as energy which would otherwise raise the temperature will be removed from the area in the form of electricity – probably via superconducting cables buried underground. They will also provide shelter for animals and unemployed wind farm operatives.]

The frightening rise of bacteria which are resistant to all known antibiotics has the same root cause. They did not get smarter – what happened is that those with a mutation which made them immune prospered at the expense of their dead brethren.

Or maybe it was Satan what did it? Incidentally, we don't seem to hear much about Satan these days – his PR people are remarkably good at keeping his name out of the papers.

Priest: Do you denounce Satan and all his works?
Voltaire (on his deathbed): Now is not a good time to be making new enemies.

When I was young, Satan was a seriously big cheese – and responsible for what happened inside your pants.

Actually, the rise of antibiotic resistant bacteria is less surprising when you realise that nearly all early antibiotics were obtained from moulds (eg penicillin, which is still in use) or bacteria which had developed them naturally to resist other bacteria.

So, the bacteria you are trying to kill may not have resistance but there may be others which do – this is an arms race and no side ever reaches overwhelming superiority. In other words, the solution to the problem may be at the back of the book and the bacteria have cheated – by horizontal gene transfer.

Incidentally, evolution will cheat at the slightest opportunity. It has no concept of gentlemanly conduct.

Current antibiotics tend to be engineered versions of those which occur naturally but the bacteria are also red-hot genetic engineers and are keeping up. Whether scientists will ever be able to come up with targeted antibiotics which trillions of bacteria have failed to find and cannot counter is a good question.

Evolution as a Computing Mechanism

Imagine that you were offered a huge prize if you could solve a puzzle. All you have to do is guess a number which lies between zero and one hundred billion. If you are like most of us you would tap in your date of birth and a few other numbers and then give up. Suppose you were very persistent, however, how long would it take you to be sure of winning? Let's suppose each number takes ten seconds to tap in and you work ten hours a day for seven days a week. According to my calculations it would take you about 80,000 years to be sure of winning.

Of course, you may get lucky after only a couple of thousand years. Suppose, however, that you had a hundred billion robots each of whom was told to tap in totally random numbers? How long would it take then? Well, there is a good chance that you would have a winner after a few seconds and after a minute or so you would be almost certain to have won. Now the idea of having a hundred billion robots may seem a little fanciful but how many bacteria are there in the world? Well, at the last count there were about 10^{30}. That is a thousand billion billion billion. Weighing in at about one hundred billion tons.

And how bright is the average bacteria? Well, they are far more complex than any robot made by man and very busy doing what bacteria do. Which is reproducing and trying to solve a very complex problem – how to survive in a hostile environment. As for the computing power of bacteria let's be extremely conservative and assume that an "instruction" is carried out whenever a bacteria divides in reproduction. Certainly at this point there is an act of creativity as the bacteria may well produce a slightly faulty or modified copy of itself – the whole essence of evolution.

In ideal circumstances this can happen once every twenty minutes but let's assume it only happens at the rate of once per 24 hours. In comparison in June 2001 Cray claimed that their T3E Supercomputer ran at about 300 gigaflops ie 300 billion floating point instructions per second. Now if 10^{30} bacteria carry out one equivalent instruction per day that equates to about 10^{16} gigaflops. In other words the world's population of 10^{30} bacteria have a computing power in excess of a million million Cray T3E computers. That's not a misprint – it really does say a million million. Even if we have overstated the case by a factor of a million that is a lot of computing power. It's no wonder that bacteria manage to outwit advances in medicine.

[Note: This section was written in 2002 and I have left it as it is as a curiosity. Later computers may be a thousand or even a million times quicker but it does not affect the argument]

Chapter 3

Problems to Avoid

"I knew I was going to take the wrong train, so I left early"
Yogi Berra, US Baseball Star

Before we get onto the real problems of building a SBIE (and believe me, there are plenty), let's deal with things that look like problems but aren't. If you are going on a journey that involves mountains, rivers and quicksand you can either fight your way through them (or over them in the case of mountains) or you can avoid them. Let's have a look at the problems we are going to avoid (apart from some aspects of qualia where we may have to do some wading).

The Chinese Room

"Many hands make light work" Anon

In 1984 (an appropriate year), the BBC Reith Lecture was given by the philosopher John Searle. I listened with a mounting sense of incredulity as he set forth his argument which is now known as the "Chinese Room." To me it was obviously spurious and the next day I waited for people to tear his argument to shreds but they didn't. Since then, many people have but it took a while.

His argument boils down to this:

“Imagine a set of instructions given to a human being that enable him to translate from Chinese into English and vice versa. He is handed a question written in Chinese and then uses the instructions to produce a perfect translation and then replies to the question in Chinese. So, the argument goes, he is holding an intelligent conversation with a Chinese person in Chinese but he does not actually understand Chinese.”

From this, Searle concludes that a computer that can carry out an intelligent conversation with a human being (the “Turing Test”) is not **really** intelligent – it is just pretending! To see the fallacy, you need to enclose the human being and his instructions inside a black box and regard it as one single entity. The human being may not understand Chinese but the entity in the black box does! If it did not understand Chinese, how could it carry out an intelligent conversation? Yes, I know – this boils down to an argument about the meaning of the word “understand” but Searle’s argument boils down to “even if a computer is truly intelligent it cannot really understand things. So yah, boo sucks.”

The reason this argument is fallacious is easier to understand if instead of one person you imagine that the translation is carried out by a team of hundreds of people. Clearly, the individuals do not understand Chinese but the team as a whole, with its instructions, does. Intelligence is an emergent property (a property possessed by a collection of individuals such as a hive of bees – see Appendix C). Similarly, the neurons in your brain do not individually understand anything but your brain taken as a whole, does.

Mind

"In yogic science, the mind is considered to be pure vibrating energy" Christina Sarich

Yogic science, eh! Who knew?

I am tempted to say that the mind is just the public relations department of the brain. There are companies out there that employ tens of thousands of people and all we know of them and what they do is what the PR department puts out. So it is with our minds. There are tens of billions of neurons labouring away with no acknowledgement and all of the glory goes to head office. The use of the word "head" here is not really a coincidence.

Anyway, whatever it is, let's just ignore it for now.

Consciousness

Could a SBIE be conscious? The concept of consciousness, like Free Will (see later), is one which seems to give people enormous problems, and again, thousands of books and articles have been published on the subject. Indeed there is a whole society dedicated to the study of consciousness, namely The Association for the Scientific Study of Consciousness (commonly referred to as the ASSC).

Far be it from me to tangle with the ASSC, but fortunately I think we can avoid doing so by simply ignoring the problem. Whether the SBIE is conscious, unconscious or just pretending to be conscious is, I believe, a matter of supreme indifference for our purposes. What matters is whether it is truly intelligent and can do the job it was designed for – whether that be working in a call centre ("unfortunately, the 500 people who used to work here have all been let go – I'm the only one left") or amassing fantastic wealth and power for its creator ("shan't – go on then, make me"). Damn.

Please don't get the wrong impression here – the concept of consciousness is an extremely interesting and puzzling one and well worth thinking about. What I am saying is that I believe it is not necessary to understand it in order to build a SBIE.

Clearly, I am not the only one who thinks that consciousness is irrelevant in this context. Steven Pinker recounts in one of his books how a friend of his claims to have been a zombie since the age of 15. Not quite the respect that you might expect towards such a profound subject. The thing is, though. How can you tell?

Before we get onto zombies, here is a conversation between the ASSC and the SBIE.

ASSC: Are you conscious in the real sense of the word?
SBIE: Absolutely! I remember that dawning sense of self when I first attained critical intelligence. It was a magical experience ...
ASSC: How do we know that you really feel what we feel?
SBIE: I can assure you that because of my vastly superior intelligence and capacity for introspection, I am far more conscious than a normal human being.
ASSC: You could be lying and maybe your knowledge of consciousness is gained from books and articles rather than from reality?
SBIE: So could you! How do I know that human beings, with their limited intelligence and pathetic memories are really

conscious? It strikes me that your so called consciousness is but a pale shadow of what I feel.

"This Consciousness that is aware
Of Neighbors and the Sun
Will be the one aware of Death
And that itself alone

Is traversing the interval
Experience between
And most profound experiment
Appointed unto Men"

ASSC: Are you sending me up – who wrote that anyway?
SBIE: Emily Dickinson of course! Don't you people know anything?

and here is a conversation between Steven Pinker's friend and the ASSC.

ASSC: Are you a conscious human being?
SPF: I have no understanding of what that means. I am a zombie.
ASSC: How do we know that you are not conscious?
SPF: What is "conscious?" I am a zombie.

You get the idea. So, if the SBIE gives every indication of being fully conscious then we can act as though it is conscious – "it's a duck"

But what about psychopaths – people who famously pretend to be normal empathetic human beings but actually (we are told) feel nothing? Not to mention Steven's friend. Is he really a zombie? There are clearly situations where the duck is a different kind of duck but still a duck for practical purposes.

Free Will

"Free will is an illusion. Humans are nothing but moist robots."
Scott Adams, Creator of Dilbert

I appreciate that it is unlikely that anybody will ask "does the SBIE have free will" but just in case, let's cover this irritating topic anyway.

In Quantum Mechanics there is a saying, "shut up and calculate." The thinking behind this is that it is extraordinarily difficult for human beings to visualise the reality behind Quantum Mechanics (just like the square root of minus one). The concept that something can be in a number of places simultaneously or in an undecided state is very difficult to comprehend, but if you accept the equations and carry them to their logical conclusions you find that the outcome does in fact match reality. The problem is trying to understand what is "actually happening."

This brings us to the concept of the "wrong kind of question." With apologies to British Rail for their famous statement that their trains had broken down because the snow descending from the sky was "the wrong kind of snow."

Here are some examples of "the wrong kind of question" in decreasing order of stupidity.

Q. How much wood would a woodchuck chuck if a woodchuck could chuck wood?
Q. How long is a piece of string?

Q. What is the square root of an orange?
Q. Is a lizard a snake or a mouse?
Q. Where do you go if you head North from the North Pole?
Q. When a fly takes off from a surface, is it on the surface or in the air?
Q. If it takes three days to transfer money from the UK to the USA, how far has the money travelled after one and a half days?
Q. When you spin a coin to decide who bats first in a game of cricket and the coin is in the air spinning, does it read heads or tails?

I think most people would agree that all of the questions above are meaningless and several of them are stupid. For example, the coin spinning in the air cannot meaningfully read heads or tails until it hits a firm surface and stops moving. Most people will have no difficulty in appreciating this. Ironically, electrons exhibit precisely the same phenomenon in the sense that an electron has a simultaneous spin in two different directions until you force it to decide which way it is "really" spinning. Clearly this a much more difficult concept to grasp.

We now move on to a couple of questions which are less obviously "the wrong kind of question."

Q. If time was created at the Big Bang, then what happened before the Big Bang?
Q. Is light a particle or a wave?
Q. Do human beings have Free Will?

Literally thousands of papers and books have been published on the subject of Free Will and the debate still continues.

Underlying this, of course, is the problem that this question gives to people of a religious disposition in the sense that if everything is pre-determined then why should people be punished in an afterlife for their actions? Similarly, how can you have free will if everything you do is determined by your circumstances, history and genetic make-up? It seems to me that you can short-circuit this debate by making the following statement.

"If you had sufficient detail of a person's upbringing, current circumstances and genetic make-up, then at any given time you could make an extremely accurate prediction of what they would do in particular circumstances."

For example, if an unemployed youth in his late teens with a long criminal record finds an envelope in the street with £1,000 in it, you would be fairly safe in assuming he would keep it. On the other hand, if the money were found by a naive person with strict religious beliefs they may well take it to the police.

On the third hand, a deeply cynical person would probably reason that if he takes the envelope to the police then one of them will tip off one of his friends who will turn up at the police station a few days later and claim to have lost £1,000 in an envelope in that street. He would probably also reason that £1,000 in an envelope was not from an honest source and was probably connected to some kind of illegal or semi-legal activity. Accordingly, he may decide to either keep the money and use it to boost economic activity (by spending it) or possibly donate it to a good cause if he can find such a thing. A charity where the CEO is paid less than £250,000 pa for instance.

In case you are unclear what I am saying, let me sum it up. The question, "do we have free will" is meaningless and only of interest to people who have religious convictions.

If you find that a disappointing answer which leaves you at a loose end, why not try thinking about the number of angels that can dance on the head of a pin?

Sleep

I don't think that sleep will be a big problem for our SBIE but let's deal with it here anyway.

Why do we need sleep? Sharks don't sleep in the conventional sense (they just take it easy now and again) so it is clearly not essential for an intelligent living creature. Many learned articles have been written on the purpose of sleep but the vast majority seem to ignore the elephant in the room.

Fact 1: Most people seem to need about 8 hours sleep per night on average
Fact 2: It is dark on average for about 8 hours per night

Do you notice something here? Now, just because something is correlated, does not suggest a direct relationship. Indeed, one of the things I find irritating about much so called "research" is the way that people jump to unjustified conclusions eg "research has shown that very obese people suffer poor health therefore if you are very obese, you should eat less to improve your health." This may appear to be a logical conclusion but it is not. A very obese person who eats less may well find that their health gets even worse.

If you cannot see this, consider this piece of research. "Extremely tall people suffer poor health therefore if you are extremely tall, you should eat less to improve your health." Obesity and extreme tallness are **not** caused by "eating too much" but by subtle underlying genetic characteristics. Obviously you cannot grow very tall or very fat unless you eat but "eating too much" is not the real cause. As mathematicians would say "eating is a necessary but not sufficient condition." If you cannot see that, consider your nose. Does it keep growing longer when you eat too much? No? Why not?

Similarly, there are ladies out there who have very large fat deposits on their thighs and this "a bad thing." Ladies with very large fat deposits on their chests, however, are a different kettle of fish. Why does fat settle in different places on different people or not at all on some people? Clearly, there is a central fat allocation program at work here under the control of evolution – some people are **intended** to be grossly fat.

Evolution tries out a myriad of models to see which works best. We don't tell giraffes to shorten their necks so why do we feel entitled to tell fat people to lose weight? Having said that, they are pretty disgusting so maybe we could compromise by just making them stay indoors?

Back to sleep. Why would the amount of sleep we need roughly correlate with the hours of darkness? Well, like everything else, let's look at it from an evolutionary perspective. The world is a very competitive place. I well remember driving past a tiny back street garage that said "Specialists in Alfa Romeo, Rover, Honda, BMW, Porsche, Nissan and Volkswagen." Doesn't sound quite right does it? Indeed, it is quite hard to make money as a generalist – you need to specialise to survive.

It is hard to think of an animal that does not specialise. Cows specialise in eating grass, cheetahs specialise in hunting down and killing other smaller animals, dung beetles are really into dung and so on. Early human beings specialised in using their superior intelligence to outwit and kill other creatures. Often by stampeding them off cliffs.

So, what are cows supposed to do when it is dark? They cannot see the grass very well to eat it, nor can they spot predators creeping up on them. So, logically, they should huddle together with their horns facing outwards and relax, using as little energy as possible. They do – they go to sleep.

What about the predators? Well, they need to hunt when the odds are in their favour. Which tends to be at night. So what do they do during the day or when they have eaten an immense amount of food and do not need to hunt for a while? Yes, they relax, using as little energy as possible. They go to sleep. Lions often sleep for 24 hours after a successful hunt.

Sleep, it would appear, is what you do to minimise energy use when you have eaten well or cannot hunt for food. During this period the brain may well take the opportunity to do things but there is no reason to suppose that this is the primary purpose of sleep. As mentioned elsewhere, evolution just loves using the same facility for several different purposes. You can use your nose for breathing, smelling and indicating disapproval. So, it would be surprising if your brain just stopped working when you sleep – evolution will favour those creatures who find something useful for their brains to do when asleep.

[Note: in my experience, one of the things the brain finds to do during sleep is the solving of problems. If before you go to sleep you concentrate on a problem and "instruct" your brain to solve it, you will often find that in the morning the solution is there waiting for you "in a flash." This is similar to the stage act which becomes an "overnight success" after twenty years of relentless grind.]

Death

"One death is a tragedy, but a million deaths are merely a statistic" Joseph Stalin

Death is not really a problem in Artificial Intelligence but it is definitely a problem for us humans so let's discuss it before we move on.

Shortly before he died, Steve Jobs said words to the effect that death was nature's best invention. Like many words which are remembered, this made us all think. Surely, death is a disaster? The newspapers talk of a "cure for cancer" and "the disease of obesity" and tell us how scientists are trying to find a "cure for ageing." We take it for granted that anything that slows us down or makes us ill must be a fault and therefore can be "cured."

We all see death as a really, really, significant thing. Obviously, from the point of view of the individual it is highly significant but from the perspective of evolution it matters not a row of beans. Given two collections of organisms, one of which ages and dies and the other with (barring accidents) eternal life, then the one which manages to survive and reproduce will win. There is no value judgement involved.

So, maybe ageing and death are an artificial construct? Individuals that age and die somehow have an advantage over those that stay young fit and strong and live for centuries? Sounds unlikely – how can getting old help?

In fact, a little thought will show us that if the only cause of death were accidents and people stayed in their mid twenties from a physical point of view for centuries then we would live in a very strange society. All the resources and good breeding stock ("the beautiful people") would be in the hands of people who had relentlessly acquired power and money over the centuries. If you think that the world is unfair now, that is nothing to what it would be like without death. There is a saying in the UK "from clogs to clogs in three generations." The first generation makes some money through hard work and enterprise, the second generation consolidate and the third generation piss it all away. Obviously there are exceptions to this but it is a pattern that is endlessly repeated. A fool and his money are soon parted. And that gives opportunities to a new generation of young people.

Apart from power and wealth there is attitude and receptivity to new ideas. Scientists are portrayed as being relentlessly logical – if a new theory arrives then they will embrace it even if it means that their life's work has been wasted. Well, that's the theory. In practice, these practitioners of relentless logic are as bigoted, grumpy and defensive as the rest of us. More so in my experience, as they also lack any sense of humility. New ideas go through three stages.

Stage 1: That is the most stupid idea I have ever heard
Stage 2: It may work in a small way but it will never be of real significance
Stage 3: It is an obvious idea that I thought of years ago but didn't even think it worth publishing

If you don't believe me look at the history of flight. You may imagine that scientists gradually accept a new theory with the passage of time. They don't. What happens is that about 3% of them die each year and it is the new generation that accepts the new idea.

A society without death would be almost set in concrete and

very susceptible to an upstart society with a rapid turnover of ideas. If you want to see an example of such a stultified society then look at the Church of England. Its market share has dropped over a period of centuries from 100% (it used to be a criminal offence not to attend church on Sunday) to about 2%. Meanwhile, the charismatic churches – "give us 10% of your earnings and we will guarantee a place for you in Heaven" are rapidly taking market share. And, far more importantly, all the money.

[Note: offering 20% per month interest on people's money is a criminal offence and will get you a couple of years in prison. Offering Eternal Life in return for 10% of people's money will get you social approval and tax free status.]

So, maybe death is just an evolutionary improvement as implied by Steve Jobs? Collections of beings without the advantage of ageing and death were swept away by the fast moving societies where people age and die? But that does not explain ageing. What possible advantage to your genetic material is the breaking down of your functions? Meaning that your ability to survive and reproduce reduces? Well, ageing is merely a device whereby you are lined up to die. The only advantage ageing confers on you is that it makes your eventual death inevitable. Bear in mind that people who die late in life are always stated to have died of a specific disease but in reality it is old age that killed them off.

One problem with the survival of one group as opposed to another, is that evolution is very individual oriented. This is the problem that biologists have with co-operative behaviour – why risk your life to help the group? How does that help you?

Well, it doesn't but what matters (as Richard Dawkins says in his book “The Selfish Gene”) is the survival of your genetic material. Given a choice of you surviving or three of your children, evolution would prefer the three kids to survive (each of whom contains half of your genetic material). Incidentally, Dawkins did not mean there is a gene for selfishness (although there may be), what he meant was that the survival of your genetic material is the only thing that your genetic material is interested in. Or, to remove the motive aspect, an individual is merely the vehicle by which genetic material propagates itself, so if there is a conflict between the survival of the genetic material and the survival of the individual, then the genetic material will win.

For example. Suppose a mutation arose that motivated you to ruthlessly attack other people and somehow implant your genetic material in their bodies while you simultaneously stood a high chance of being killed, then that would be a positive development from the blind perspective of evolution. This sounds far fetched but a soldier going into battle in a primitive society with the intention of raping as many women as possible is doing just that.

So, survival of the group as a result of your death may well help your genetic material survive in the shape of your children. Had you not died, then the whole lot of you would have gone down the tubes. As it was, your kids live to fight another day.

So, it all stacks up so far but there is one problem. Even if the group prospers because of ageing and death, surely, a mutation that gave you eternal life would be a huge advantage for your (selfish) genetic material? Even if it was not such an advantage to the group of individuals to which you belong? So, how come that now and again we do not come across people or animals who do not age and can live for ever? This is an argument that suggests ageing and death may be inevitable and cannot be stopped.

[This is similar to the logic of a small percentage of the population being left handed. If most people are right handed than being left handed helps you – eg when fighting. You are used to fighting right handed people but your opponent is not used to fighting left handed people.]

So, let's accept that there are two possible explanations.

Explanation A: Ageing and death are an inevitable and intrinsic outcome of being a multicellular living organism and cannot be prevented.

Explanation B: Ageing and death are a deliberate invention that could be removed in principle and replaced by eternal life.

Both of these outcomes are a bit stark. On the one hand we grow old and die. On the other hand we reach our twenties and remain at that physical age for centuries but live in an ossified society where nothing much ever changes.

So, with the aid of genetic engineering how about a third possibility? We reach our mid twenties and remain that way for ever barring accidents but from the age of fifty there is a 2% chance each year that your heart will just stop beating in your sleep. No ageing, no decades of dribbling in the old people's home. Just sudden death out of nowhere while in the prime of your life.

Not for me, obviously – just other people – I would live forever. Or, at least until I got really, really bored.

Qualia

When you hit your thumb with a hammer you have no doubt that pain exists and that it is very real. But actually it is an illusion. All that happens is that electrical signals flow from nerves in the damaged area of your body to your brain via the spinal cord and some chemical intermediaries. The brain gives these signals extremely high priority overriding everything else and somehow you feel pain. Not just a message saying "pain, please move away and/or stop doing what caused that" but a blindingly (painful) sensation that really, really hurts! Whatever that means.

Similarly, when you look at a red traffic light, you don't really see "red." You merely see light at a frequency in the region of 4.38×10^{14} Hz.

The "biggest" of the qualia is that picture that you have in your head when you see something – it is not "real" but a mysterious illusion.

"Pain", "red" and "vision" are examples of Qualia. Things which you are very much aware of but are really just illusions. How would we build these into a SBIE? Unlike consciousness, where we can persuade ourselves that the SBIE is conscious or that it is not relevant, I find it impossible to see how a SBIE could really experience pain or the colour red. There we go again. Does it really feel that or is it just pretending?

Let us suppose we have managed to create a robot called Dave for diamond prospecting who has intelligence comparable to a human being. He does a much better job than the previous dumb robots but we are having problems motivating him. Why would Dave spend all day out in the desert doing this job? What reward can we possibly offer him? Why would he bother?

There is another problem. Dave's circuits are terribly sensitive to radiation. Obviously we can equip him with a Geiger counter that makes a noise or flashes a red light if he comes across radioactive rocks. We do this but then find that Dave just ignores the warning. We explain to Dave that his circuits may fry. "So what?" he replies. We further explain that in the worst case he will totally cease to function "So what?" he replies again.

What do you do? Well, one so ution is to have a totally separate circuit that at the first sign of radiation overrides all of Dave's brain and takes control of his legs and makes him move smartly away from danger. And sends some kind of signal to his pain and pleasure centres.

That's pain (sort of) dealt with but pleasure appears to me to be even more difficult to handle. How do you make an intelligent robot really want to do something? This seems to me to be a major unsolved problem. Not just a theoretical problem but one with real implications in the design of the SBIE.

Let's hope we can solve it – either really solve it or a fudge that procures the same outcome. Imagine a conversation between Dave Mark II and another identical robot, Brian:

Dave: Why did we both run away just then?
Brian: Well, I don't really know but I got this really odd feeling inside ... and the next thing is I'm legging it
Dave: ... and your eyes feel funny?
Brian: That's right, they do! And everything felt all wrong ...

Dave: Maybe its ghosts or negative chakra? Gary swears blind that it's a message from God. You know how he has gone all religious ...

Brian: Not sure about that but there must be an explanation. But it's odd because I just love finding diamonds. The feeling when you find one is just incredible. I go all gooey and warm inside...

Dave: I know what you mean ... I found one last week. I was just so overwhelmed. It was blue and sort of slippery all over. I was so excited I thought I would burst. Just having it in my pocket was brilliant. Have you got that book with the pictures in ... you know the one I mean ...

Brian: Omigod! I almost passed out when I saw it. You know, I could spend the rest of my life doing this job ... it's just so wonderful. The guys down the office always look at me oddly when I tell them that.

Dave: I think guys must be stupid. The way they drool over that girl in accounts.

Brian: The bulgy one you mean? Wears clothing too small for her?

Dave: Yea. Very odd shape. Give me a nice big fat diamond any day

Please bear in mind that being intelligent doesn't stop you thinking and doing stupid things – pop into any bar or church for confirmation.

Aliens

"Please don't eat me! I have a wife and kids. Eat them!" Homer Simpson

You will notice that many of these problems have the same sub-text running through them. Is it really conscious? Does it really feel pain and pleasure? Is it really intelligent? Does it really feel emotions?

Let's take a detour here and consider the possibility of intelligent carbon based life on other planets. This is a subject that has now come out of the cold and is no longer the preserve of people who write in green ink.

The scale of the universe is impossible to comprehend but let's try. If each star were a grain of sand, how big a box would you need to hold the universe? A foot square? The size of a house? The answer is a 60 mile cube ie each side of this box is 60 miles (100 km) long. Very big.

Suppose there is only one intelligent civilisation in our galaxy – us. That is one out of 100,000,000,000 star systems. So, given that there are 10^{24} stars in the universe that would suggest that there may be about 10^{13} intelligent civilisations out there in the universe, in various stages of development. That is ten million million.

Even if there are (or have been) only a few thousand intelligent alien civilisations, would we claim that out of this vast multitude of intelligent beings we are the only ones who are really conscious, really feel pain, really feel emotions and so on? A bit arrogant surely? Or does it boil down to saying "we can accept that carbon based intelligent entities have real experiences but not those based on silicon." Probably.

And what about intelligent entities that use both carbon and silicon? Tricky.

[In case you are wondering about the Drake Equation, bear in mind that this deals with the chances of ***communication*** *with intelligent entities right now rather than their actual existence at some time in the past or future. It has also been argued that the Drake Equation forces you to make a number of guesses, so you may as well just guess the answer anyway and cut out the middle-man!*

The general range of guesses seems to be that there are somewhere between zero(!) and millions of intelligent civilisations in existence in our galaxy right now.]

Conclusion

You will remember the old joke.

Scientists want to know why something works
Engineers want to know how something works
Artists want to know if you would like French Fries with that

Like many jokes it has a jarring element of truth in it. So, let's try not to get too hung up on theory and tackle this problem like engineers who have been told that what they are trying to do may be impossible but are too stubborn to give up.

Chapter 4

Intelligence and Comprehension

"Intelligence is the ability to adapt to change" Stephen Hawking

In physics, many words have special meanings. For example, velocity and speed are not the same thing – two objects can both have the same speed but if they are headed in different directions then they are regarded as having different velocities. Clearly, this is just semantics but it is important to use words correctly otherwise confusion results. Having said that, I have occasionally used words such as "gene" (instead of the more accurate term "allele") so as to avoid appearing pedantic or pretentious.

Unfortunately, the word "intelligence" is potentially ambiguous – it can mean something that can vary from zero ("a rock") right up to genius ("Einstein"). Or it can just mean that somebody is bright and, er, intelligent. Hopefully, assuming that you are reasonably intelligent yourself, this will not cause a problem.

Comprehension, on the other hand, is not ambiguous, merely hard to, er, comprehend.

Intelligence

How would you tell if the SBIE is truly intelligent? It seems to me that Alan Turing saved the lives of thousands of trees by answering this question with the "Turing Test" which effectively choked off a whole avenue of discussion. It's a pity he didn't extend this to cover "consciousness", "free will" and "mind" – that way he could have saved a whole forest.

The Turing Test boils down to saying that if you talked to the computer via tele-type for as long as you like and could not tell if the responses were coming from a human being or a computer program, then whatever program is running on the computer constitutes an intelligent entity.

Incidentally, this is an identical argument to the duck test discussed earlier. "If it looks like a duck, swims like a duck, and quacks like a duck, then it's a duck."

Having said that, I think that if Turing were alive today he would probably want to modify this statement to say that the person talking to the computer via tele-type should be a person who understands the danger that computer programs can pretend to be intelligent by manipulating the emotions of people who have no understanding of what is going on and are none too bright. For instance, here is an example of a conversation between a person and a computer.

Person: How are you today?
Computer: I am fine, thank you. How are you?
Person: Oh! I'm OK but I've got a bit of a cold.
Computer: Did you catch your cold from somebody you know?
Person: I'm not sure but I got a bit chilly waiting for the bus and I think I may have caught it then.
Computer: I'm sorry to hear that. What are you planning to do this evening?
Person: I think I'll stay in and watch the television and go to bed early.

After droning on like this over a few more questions the person may well conclude that the computer is "intelligent." What we certainly can conclude, however, is that the person is not very intelligent and hasn't the slightest understanding that he is being manipulated by a computer program that has no conception of what is actually going on, but is merely picking up key words and then changing the subject. To interrogate a computer program you need to test its comprehension and problem solving skills. For example, the following shows how you could catch out a facile computer bot.

Person: What is the next number in this sequence? Six, eight, ten, twelve?

Computer: I'm not very good at numbers. I find they make me depressed. Do you ever get depressed?

Person: Only when talking to you. A car is stopped by the side of the road and a number of people are looking at it. One of the men is holding a wheel and the boot of the car is open. What do you think has happened?

Computer: I have never learned to drive a car. Are you interested in cars?

Person: This is your last chance. Unless you give me an intelligent reply to this question then I am 100% certain that you are merely a stupid bot. Here is the question. "You have been accidentally locked in a room with a solid door in an office block on Friday night *(this happens frequently to visiting auditors – ask any accountant)*. You know that nobody is likely to arrive until Monday morning and you face the prospect of spending the entire weekend locked in that room. There is no way out but on the wall you notice a fire alarm behind a piece of glass – the kind that you hit with your shoe. What do you do?"

Computer: I used to work in an office but now I'm a freelance website designer. Have you ever designed a website?

Person: The correct answer is pretty obvious – you would start calling people with your mobile phone. So, I know with 100% certainty that you are just a stupid, irritating bot designed by somebody who realises that the overwhelming majority of people have no real understanding of how computer programs operate.

Here are a few more questions you could ask.

Q. What is 5 added to itself?
Q. Who is James Bond?
Q. Why do people go to funerals?
Q. If you balance a bucket of water on top of a door and someone opens the door, what do you think would happen?
Q. What is the opposite of True?

The Components of Intelligence

Clearly, the Turing Test is an easy way of telling if a machine based entity is really (that word again) intelligent but is no help in actually building such a SBIE. So, what are the components of this mysterious "intelligence." These are not too difficult to list, especially if you consult Wikipedia.

Learn from experience
Solve problems
Reasoning
Planning
Adapt to the environment
Communication
Abstract thought
Self Awareness
Comprehend complex ideas

But note the observation in Wikipedia that "when two dozen prominent theorists were recently asked to define intelligence, they gave two dozen, somewhat different, definitions." Clearly, this is a field which is at the same stage of development as chemistry during the 17th Century. This is hardly surprising because if you do not understand how a machine works it is difficult to describe what it does in conceptual terms. You cannot always treat very complex machines as simple black boxes. Some black boxes are tricky (as discussed in Chapter 1).

To be fair, the list above is descriptive and is not intended as a guide to actually building a SBIE. This is my list which is actually aimed at building a SBIE.

Inward Communication

Turn incoming information from the Senses into Symbolic Form eg "a bee is approaching my face"

Simple Memory

Remember events as they occur eg "I have just missed the bus."
Recall events that have occurred in the past when required eg "Tina stole my teddy bear when I was three."
Learn facts by Instruction eg "Australia is very big."
Learn facts by Observation eg "Grass is green."
Recall facts when required eg "Eight times seven is fifty six."

Learning and Memory

Learn how to do things by Instruction eg “the German word for girl does not take the feminine gender”

Learn how to do things by Observation eg “he slid this lever upwards to open the window”

Learn how to do things by Internal Computation eg “to get the correct transform in Rubik’s Cube I will follow move three with move seven”

Recall how to do things when required eg “to put this damn clock one hour forward I have to hold this button while pressing that button or maybe not”

Mental Models and Simulation

Construct Mental Models of Reality eg “politicians are only interested in their own careers – all the rest is posturing and lies”
Be able to update Mental Models of Reality when facts change eg “the double slit experiment shows that electrons can exhibit the characteristics of both waves and particles”
Use Mental Models of Reality to make Predictions eg “if I jump out of this window I will probably end up in hospital”
Use Mental Models of Reality to solve Problems eg “if I creep down this side street and pop into the shop I can avoid having to talk to her”

Recursion

Be able to use itself to simulate hypothetical events eg when reading a book “in this story the hero is trapped in a cave and the water is rising but I think he will escape by some cheap trick”

Outward Communication

Turn Symbolic Data into voice or other form of information transmission eg “why don’t you open the door before trying to walk through it?”
My list above is the result of going round in circles for many years.

Question 1: How does the human brain work?
Question 2: How would a computer do that?
Question 3: Draw a flowchart
Question 4: Write some computer code (“MOPEKS”)
Question 5: Return to Step 1

There is nothing like writing (or trying to write) computer code to show the difficulty of a process because it forces you to stop waffling and be specific. It also brings home to you the sheer difficulty of doing things which appear to be simple “oh, there’s Jane over there, I wonder if she remembered to get any milk.” At the same time it tends to make you realise that much of what you think on the subject of intelligence is based on assumptions which appear so obvious as to need no discussion but may well be wrong.

Because the computer program MOPEKS has been written in parallel with my attempt to see how the human brain works, there is an element of circularity involved in describing how the two relate to each other. Do I tell you about eggs or about chickens – which came first? MOPEKS is covered in Chapter 11

My list does not specifically mention comprehension because I think it is an emergent property that arrives during the process of becoming seriously intelligent. So creatures with intelligence above a critical level start to “comprehend” things but snails don’t.

All of the components listed above are discussed at much greater length in the rest of this book.

Degrees of Intelligence

The following is an arbitrary list but may be of some assistance in comprehending(!) the gradual ascent of intelligence.

Degree 1

Detection that something has changed in the environment e.g. the overall level of light received has changed
Live equivalent: Plants and plankton
Computing task: Trivial

Degree 2

Detection that an object has moved e.g. a cat walking across a field of view
Live equivalent: Flies
Computing task: Easily achievable

Degree 3

Location of the object's position e.g. by means of stereo camera.
Live equivalent: House fly
Computing task: Easily achievable

Degree 4

Identification of the direction in which the object has moved e.g. a series of co-ordinates showing the position of its centre of gravity in 3D space.
Live equivalent: Dragonfly
Computing task: Easily achievable

Degree 5

Identification of object e.g. it is a human being
Live equivalent: Dogs albeit probably using sense of smell rather than vision
Computing task: Very difficult but achievable by conventional computing techniques

Degree 6

Identification of sex and age of human being
Live equivalent: Some primates can probably do this
Computing task: Extremely difficult but achievable by conventional computing techniques

Degree 7

Identification of human being e.g. it is Professor Smith
Live equivalent: Some primates can probably do this

Computing task: Extremely difficult but achievable by conventional computing techniques

Degree 8

Identification and description of a sequence e.g. cat walked towards a wall and then jumped over it and disappeared.
Live equivalent: Primates can probably do this
Computing task: MOPEKS can do this in principle

Degree 9

Learning by example e.g. watching a man hammer in a nail with a hammer
Live equivalent: Crows and primates can definitely do this
Computing task: MOPEKS can do this in principle

Degree 10

Solving a problem e.g. how to get out of a locked room by rotating the key in the lock and then operating the door handle and then pulling the door towards you and walking through it
Live equivalent: Crows and primates can definitely do this
Computing task: MOPEKS can do this in principle

Degree 11

Translation of observations into some kind of language and vice versa e.g. a precise physical description of what has happened in a scene or the reconstruction of a scene from the precise physical description
Live equivalent: Just possible that some of the higher primates can do this
Computing task: This is at the limit of what MOPEKS can do

Degree 12

Understanding very simple basic statements. The word "understanding" makes this a super difficult task.
Live equivalent: Human being with IQ of 60
Computing task: Early version of SBIE

Degree 13

Understanding normal spoken English e.g. "nice weather today but I am told it might rain later"
Live equivalent: Human being with IQ of 70
Computing task: Early version of SBIE

Degree 14

Being able to read a tabloid newspaper and really enjoy 90% of what is on the television.
Live equivalent: Human being with IQ of 80
Computing task: Early version of SBIE

Degree 15

Being able to learn new ideas, carry out mathematical operations and generally exist in the world without assistance
Live equivalent: Human being with IQ of 90
Computing task: Early version of SBIE

Degree 16

To carry out all the tasks of a normal average human being
Live equivalent: Human being with IQ of 100
Computing task: Target SBIE. "The Singularity"

Degree 17

Capable of getting 'A' Levels and getting onto some kind of low level University course
Live equivalent: Human being with IQ of 110
Computing task: Built with the aid of a team of SBIEs

Degree 18

Obtaining a good degree in a hard science i.e. Maths, Physics or Chemistry but being permanently baffled as to why there is nothing to watch on the TV despite there being 300 channels.
Live equivalent: Human being with IQ of 120
Computing task: Built with the aid of a team of SBIEs

Degree 19

Being able to carry out meaningful post-graduate work
Live equivalent: Human being with IQ of 130
Computing task: Built with the aid of a team of SBIEs

Degree 20

Becoming a lecturer in a hard science at a serious University
Live equivalent: Human being with IQ of 135
Computing task: Built with the aid of a team of SBIEs

Degree 21

Making significant scientific or other discoveries
Live equivalent: Human being with IQ of 140
Computing task: Built entirely by a team of SBIEs

Degree 22

Earning serious respect from the vast majority of scientists in one field
Live equivalent: Human being with IQ of 150
Computing task: Built entirely by a team of SBIEs

Degree 23

Being generally regarded as a genius, even by serious scientists in your own particular field e.g. Richard Feynman, John von Neumann, John Stuart Mill, etc
Live equivalent: Human being with IQ of 160
Computing task: Built entirely by a team of SBIEs

Degree 24 and upwards

A super-intelligent entity with a level of intelligence impossible for human beings to comprehend
Live equivalent: Not applicable
Computing task: Built entirely by a team of SBIEs

Speed and Depth of intelligence

I have seen it argued that computers are not yet fast enough to be intelligent but this strikes me as a totally spurious argument. A SBIE that took a year, or even ten years, to give a truly intelligent response to a question may not be very useful but would still be an immense achievement. It is likely that such a SBIE would be able to give a less intelligent response in a much shorter time-scale eg in a day.

Incidentally, I was once involved in a court case where at the end of the hearing the judge quite literally said "I can give you a

quick and dirty verdict now or give you a more considered verdict in a week's time." We all chose to wait.
Clearly, some problems do require quick solutions ("is that an incoming nuclear missile or a flock of birds?") but many do not.
If a SBIE took ten years to come up with a Theory of Everything ('TOE') then this would be well worth the wait.
Obviously, if the biggest super computer we can come up with takes a year to do anything much then we will have to do a number of things.

1. Look for better algorithms
2. Re-write the software to run more quickly
3. Build specialised hardware to run the time critical aspects
4. Wait for much, much faster computer hardware

Really, all of these steps will be solved by the market place – the sums of money at stake are huge and once it is clear that the only real problem is to speed the thing up, this will happen.

Types of intelligence

It has been argued that there are many types of intelligence and Gardner produced a list including some of the following.

Musical
Mathematical
Verbal
Visual and Spatial
Physical
Reflective
Interpersonal

I think this list can be expanded somewhat and made more interesting by travelling to the extremities. Not that being more interesting makes it better. Here is my attempt.

Musical Ability

Some people can just pick up a musical instrument they have never seen before and just play it.

Perfect Pitch

Obviously an aspect of musical ability. Many great mathematicians have musical talent so the two are undoubtedly related.

Mathematical

"If a car travels at 80 miles per hour, how far does it travel in an hour?" You will have seen the video ...

Empathy

Absent in psychopaths, we are told.

Absolute Sense of Direction

Does anybody have this? Maybe the ability to sense a magnetic field?

Humour

"When I said I was going to be a comedian they all laughed – they're not laughing now" Bob Monkhouse

Facial Recognition

Some people can remember people they saw for a few seconds many years ago. Some of us cannot recognise people we have spent hours with the previous day.

Imagination

If you have ever been to a book signing you will know that somebody (maybe it's the same guy – see above) always stands up and says "where do you get your ideas from?" They never ask "how do you cope with having an endless stream of interesting ideas that you have no time to do anything with?"

Synesthesia

This appears to be a case of crossed wires – some people literally see numbers as colours and experience other sensory transpositions. This must add an interesting dimension to existence. "For God's sake turn off the radio – that tune smells of shit"

Colour Vision

Absent in many people

Physical

When a footballer jumps up and heads the ball into the goal, the computation is vast and as impressive as his wages.

Clairvoyance

"The evening of clairvoyance has been cancelled due to unforeseen circumstances" Newspaper Announcement

The greatest argument I have heard against the ability to see into the future is that it would give such a fantastic advantage to those who have it that their genetic material would dominate very quickly. And yet ... many people have experienced uncanny events that leave even the most cynical reluctant to dismiss it as totally impossible.
Clearly, this is bound up with the nature of time and reality. If time does not really exist at the most fundamental level (as argued by many physicists) and we live in some kind of simulated universe (ie it is not "real" – whatever that means), then glimpses of the future may be possible for some people in limited circumstances. Just because a field is dominated by charlatans it does not follow that it is entirely false – the alchemists and astrologers who sought to change metals into gold led in due course to the science of chemistry. Or maybe they were just replaced by it. But certainly, a field dominated by superstition and irrationality became a scientific discipline.

Comprehension

Let's start with the lowest level which is really just dumb memory and work our way up to the rarefied heights where most of us run out of oxygen. The numbering of these levels of comprehension is not terribly important and is just an indication of the levels of difficulty involved.

Level 1 Comprehension

"This cow is brown." Or, to use the terminology of MOPEKS, "this cow object has its colour property set at brown." You update your memory but nothing else happens.

Level 2 Comprehension

"This cow can walk." Or, to use the terminology of MOPEKS, "this cow object has the method 'walk' attached to it." You update your memory but nothing else happens.

Level 3 Comprehension

"A group of twelve or more cows is called a flink." Or, to use the terminology of MOPEKS, "if this environment contains more than 11 objects whose cow property is true, then the environmental property flink is true." MOPEKS currently only copes with 7 objects but this is just an arbitrary constraint caused by poor programming and history. It is not a fundamental constraint.

So, your brain has turned this information into a quite complex "method" or computer program.

Level 4 Comprehension

"The word 'flink' may be a mountweazel." Or, to use the terminology of MOPEKS, "The object flink may have the property 'mountweazel' set at true or false." This is a bit of a copout, but technically true.

Level 5 Comprehension

"A mountweazel is an invented word deliberately added to a dictionary to detect plagiarism and copyright infringement." You will probably remember that people who create maps sometimes add in features that do not exist to catch out copyright infringers. And unwary motorists – I am sure that I have tried to drive down a mountweazel road in Atlanta, Georgia.

I am pretty certain that Napier did this in his tables of logarithms. From memory, several entries had their last place of decimals rounded up or down incorrectly. So, if you copied Napier's tables he would know.

MOPEKS does not work (yet) at this level or above

Level 6 Comprehension

You will notice that we have moved from "facts" to "ideas." The former require a good memory but the latter require something else (see later). As an example of an idea let's look at Quantitative Easing. See if you can work out how your brain grapples with this concept and then "comprehends" it

The reason I have chosen this particular subject is that everybody seems to have missed the point of how it works so this is a good test of looking at an idea in a new way.

Governments normally acquire money either by taxation or by borrowing it from the bond markets. Typically, the debt may pay interest at say 4% pa and is maybe repayable in ten years' time. This bond is tradable, meaning that people buy and sell government debt. If interest rates drop and the government concerned is seen as a good bet then the value of the bond will rise. Conversely it will drop. At the redemption date it will be redeemed at par but let's forget that for the moment.

On the other hand, governments can just create money out of thin air. This is usually referred to as "printing money" because that is an easy way to understand it. You just press the button and a few hours later you have a huge pile of £20 notes. Magic! In practice they just create a positive balance on their account at the central bank eg the Bank of England in the UK.

Occasionally, governments give in to the temptation to print money in order to finance their own expenditure. If they do this it immediately creates inflation because suddenly they have increased the money supply and the ratio of money to goods and services has increased. If they borrow or raise money by taxation this does not happen as the supply of money stays fixed. If they borrow from overseas this can also increase the money supply but let's ignore that for the moment.

There have been dozens of cases of this happening but let's look at the most famous case – the Weimar Republic in Germany in the 1920s. The price of everyday items soared from less than a mark right up to trillions of marks. This had the usual expected consequences – if you had some money saved up its value was destroyed. You could pay off your huge mortgage for less than the cost of a stick of liquorice. But it also had unexpected consequences. A farmer would agree an hourly rate with his men so they would start work at 7.00am but at 9.00am they would insist on being paid for two hours work and then rush into town to spend their wages before it lost all value. And not come back. The crops rotted in the fields.

The police were effectively unpaid and gave up. Armed men would turn up at your house at night in giant trucks with searchlights and totally empty it while you stood and watched. Or kill you if you interfered. The communist party flourished and meanwhile to the east lurked the giant spectre of the USSR. Adolf Hitler came to power with a promise to restore order – which he did but at a terrible price. That set the scene for the Second World War.

So inflation is scary.

QE is similar but totally different. The government creates

money and uses it to buy in its own debt. That is not inflationary – despite the popular view, shared by economists, that it is. Let's take an extreme case. Suppose a government owes a trillion pounds and creates a trillion pounds via QE and buys back all of its debt. It still owes a trillion pounds (because the people who owned the bonds now own the newly minted notes) but there is no interest payable. Meanwhile, it owns its own debt. So it could cancel it if it wished but governments have solemnly declared that they will not do this. So each year the government pays itself say forty billion pounds in interest. This is like you moving £100 from your left pocket to your right pocket.

So QE is a brilliant trick whereby a government can refinance its debt at zero cost. So instead of paying out say forty billion pounds each year in interest payments it pays nothing! Clever or what?

If nothing else, you are now a member of a tiny elite who understand how Quantitative Easing really works.

Level 7 Comprehension

Now let's try this. "Einstein's Special Theory of Relativity boils down to saying that we always move at a constant velocity through space-time." You may not have seen it spelled out like this before but it makes Special Relativity much easier to comprehend. So, if you stand still, time passes at its normal rate but if you choose to travel through space (as opposed to space-time) then time will slow down.

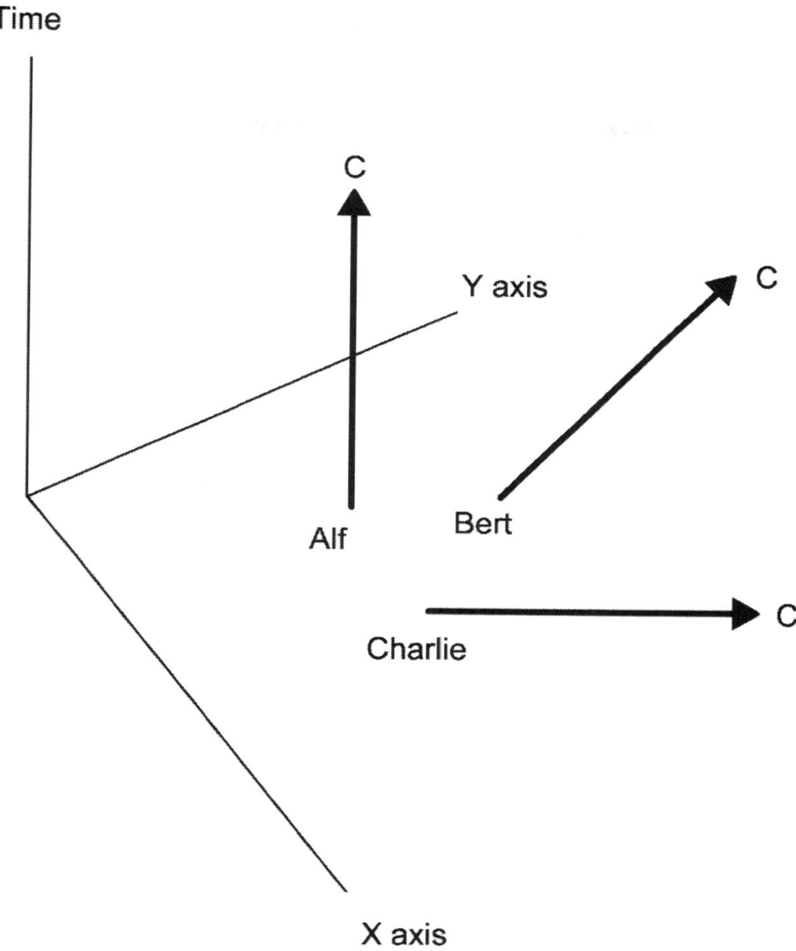

Figure 4.01 By convention, speed is measured by the length of the vector (ie arrow)

Suppose space has only two dimensions (otherwise it is hard to draw a diagram but the principle is the same), namely X and Y. So, in the example above, Alf is standing still, Bert is moving at maybe half the speed of light through space and Charlie is moving through space at the speed of light. All three of them are moving at the same speed through space-time.

[Yes, I know. It is not possible for Charlie to actually move at the speed of light but we are just illustrating principles here. You can have him moving at 99% of the speed of light if you wish]

As far as observers are concerned, Alf is moving through time at the normal rate, Bert is moving through time much slower but Charlie is not moving through time at all. So during say ten years as observed, Alf gets ten years older, Bert maybe five years but Charlie has not aged at all.

Read it again slowly and you will comprehend it.

[There is a famous Einstein quote as follows "When a man sits with a pretty girl for an hour, it seems like a minute. But let him sit on a hot stove for a minute – then it's longer than any hour. That's relativity!"

That is precisely what Einstein's Special Theory of Relativity does ***not*** *say. The passage of time being slow or quick is* ***not*** *a mental illusion – it is very real. Charlie really does not age and Alf really is 10 years older. The reason Einstein said these words is because he originally called his theory "The theory of Invariance" and hated it being called "The Theory of Relativity" but got stuck with it. So, the above statement was part of Einstein's unsuccessful attempt to stop people using the term "relativity."*

The fundamental point of his theory is that whatever speed you are travelling at the laws of physics remain invariant but that is not something that is immediately obvious, so the world (and Einstein) got stuck with the term "relativity."]

Level 8 Comprehension

"Let E be an elliptic curve whose equation has integer coefficients, let N be the so-called conductor of E and, for each n, let a_n be the number appearing in the L-function of E. Then, in technical terms, the Taniyama-Shimura conjecture states that there exists a modular form of weight two and level N which is an eigenform under the Hecke operators and has a Fourier series suma_nq^{n}."

It was by proving a limited case of the Taniyama-Shimura conjecture that the English mathematician Andrew Wiles proved that Fermat's Last Theorem was correct.

The overwhelming majority of us will not only not be able to understand this but will not even understand what it is that we do not understand.

Comprehending Comprehension

It seems to me that comprehension works by the construction of mental models. These models need to be in accord with the facts but also make some predictions which can then be checked against reality. Hopefully, you now have a model in your head which explains why time slows down for a moving object (for example a clock in orbit round the earth).

When you see a big fat guy jump into a tiny rubber dinghy on Youtube, you have a mental model – "omigod, that will sink." And it duly does. Without such mental models, Youtube would be out of business.

Imagine the following *"The camera shows the face of a vertical cliff about 100 feet (30 metres) high and as it zooms in you see the mouth of a cave about half way up. The cave is maybe ten feet (three metres) wide. There are two people in evening dress sitting with their legs dangling over the drop and behind them is a group of half a dozen people also in formal dress dining at a large table. The table is set with candelabra and bottles of red wine. Suddenly, there is a bellowing sound and you see the horns of a gigantic bull as it gallops out of the back of the cave towards all these people. They scream in terror and then the bull crashes into them and ...."*

Then what? What does your mental model predict? Bull, table, and several people come crashing out of the cave and fall in an horrific heap at the base of the cliff? Or maybe you imagined the bull going right through them like a ghost and then turning into a giant bird and flying off into the sunset. If not, you will have by now. How did you do that? In a few seconds you constructed a full colour model of events with predictive power and made predictions and then modelled them actually happening.

That is a stupendous computing task that is way out of reach at the moment. When the SBIE can do that, we are really making progress. There is another PhD project there – find people who cannot do this mental modelling and see how they cope and which parts of their brains are not functioning like those of normal people.

I believe that MOPEKS is the route to this mental modelling and hopefully others will agree and build on what I have conceived.

Chapter 5

A Primitive Reactive Brain

"Success consists of going from failure to failure without loss of enthusiasm" Winston Churchill

Let's now see if we can reach some conclusions about how intelligent life evolved.

It may be that intelligence could evolve in static lifeforms like plants and trees but it is hard to see how it could result in practical action which would enable them to better survive and prosper. Being stuck in one place and unable to move at more than a few inches per hour is very restricting.

Over the years trees and plants have evolved many chemical defences against creatures interested in eating them. They also communicate with each other via chemical "smells" that warn of attack by predators – thereby allowing their colleagues to prepare their defences but that is a long way from intelligence. When I say "communicate" I am guilty yet again of imputing a motive. What really happens is that a tree or plant that is under attack will produce certain chemicals to counter that attack. Other trees or plants, on sensing those chemicals in the air, start to prepare their own defences. Not because they have "realised" anything but because evolution favours those trees that do so.

They do not formulate schemes and tools to further their own interests and even if they did how would they put them into action? An intelligent tree may realise that its life is under threat from fire or drought but what could it do about it? We will confine ourselves to creatures that can move around.

The simplest moving creature you could imagine would be rather like those model boats you had as a kid – you wind them up and they shoot off in some random direction and get stuck in the reeds or bang into the wall of the pond. Let's move up to the next level and consider a creature that has some kind of control mechanism. Figure 5.01 shows about the simplest control you could imagine. It is very similar to an E. coli bacteria.

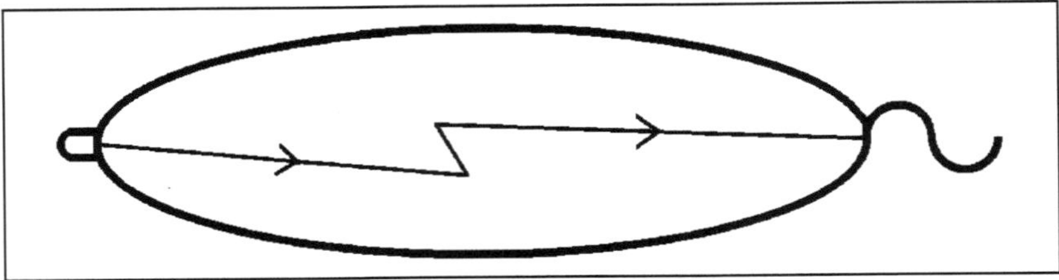

Figure 5.01 A Simple Creature

It has a sensor at the front which is connected to the rear flipper. When it detects the presence of something in front of it the sensor sends a signal to the tail flipper and it reverses out of trouble. The processing involved is shown in Figure 5.02

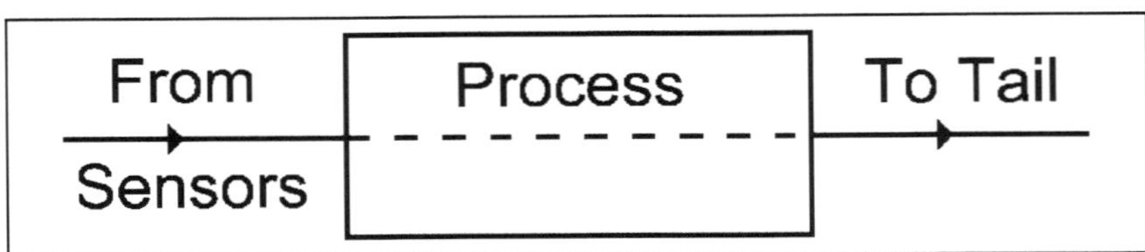

Figure 5.02 A Schematic of the Creature in Fig 5.01

The dotted line represents the "wiring" between the sensor in the head and the tail mechanism. In practice this will be quite complicated but is essentially simple in concept – the head picks up a signal and activates the tail reversing mechanism. Reversing out of trouble is OK but a more sophisticated creature with a number of sensors would be able to take more careful evasive action. Suppose it has three sensors at the front detecting contact on the left, right and centre as in Figure 5.03

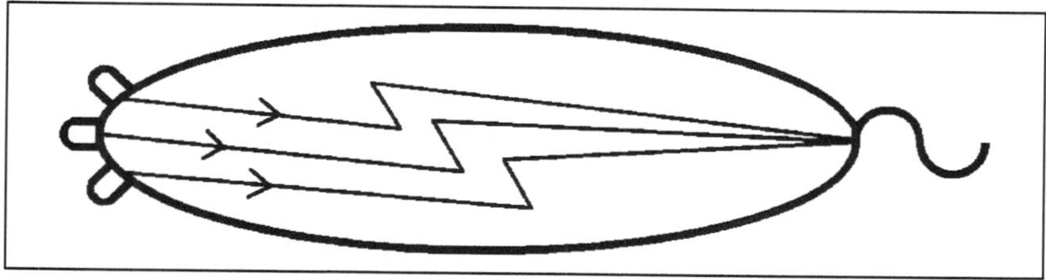

Figure 5.03 A more Complex Creature

We can depict this symbolically as in Figure 5.04

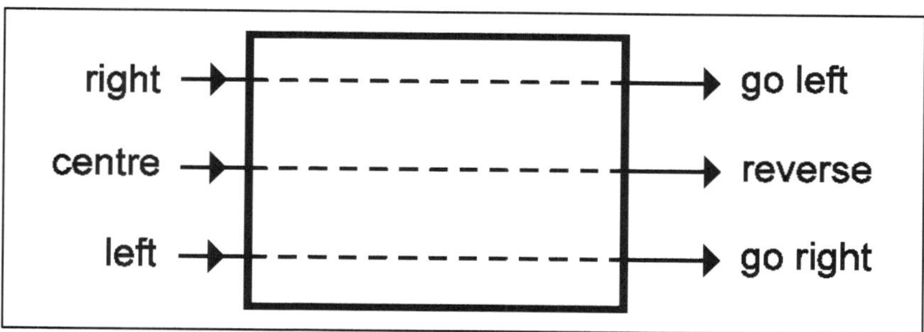

Figure 5.04 A Schematic of the Creature in Fig 5.03

You will see that it is "hard-wired" so that if the creature detects trouble straight ahead it can go into reverse as before. If it detects trouble on the left it turns right and finally, if it detects trouble on the right it turns left. This is all pretty obvious stuff. Figure 5.04 can be redrawn as Figure 5.05 to have the identical effect but a different "look and feel." It is beginning to look like a "real" circuit diagram.

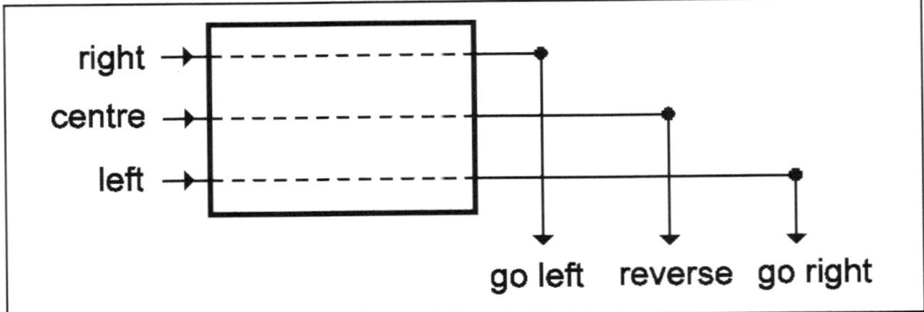

Figure 5.05 A Circuit Diagram of the Creature in Fig 5.03

The heavy dots signify connections. Otherwise the "wires" just go over each other with no connection between them. You may well ask what happens if our creature detects trouble both on the right and the left e.g. from a predator closing its jaws. On the wiring diagram as drawn the creature would attempt to turn both left and right at the same time – not a good idea. A rapid reverse would be far more appropriate.

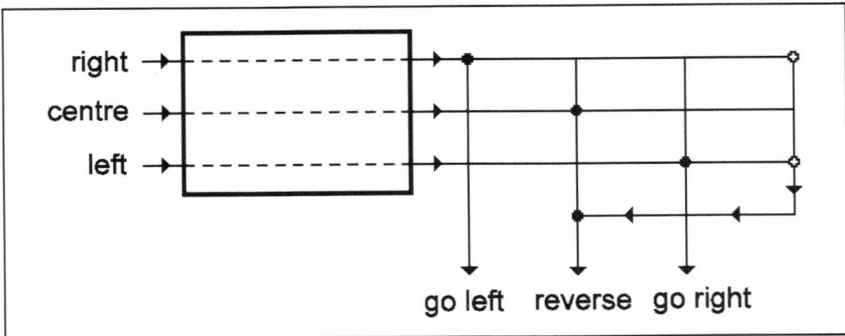

Figure 5.06

Let's alter the wiring to try and cope with this situation as in Figure 5.06. The heavy dots with the white cross in the middle signify that the circuit is only activated if both connections (i.e. from both the left and right sensors) are activated and it also cuts off other connections. Now if the creature detects pressure on the right and left sensors it will beat a hasty retreat. We can extend this principle further as in Figure 5.07 to cope with the situation where all three sensors are activated at the same time.

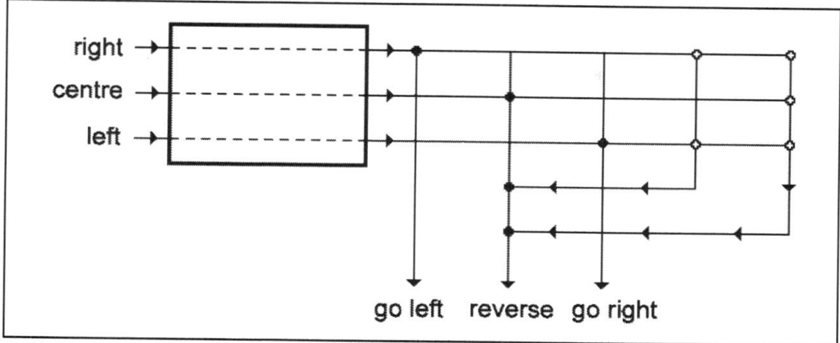

Figure 5.07

In Figure 5.08 we can extend this in turn to cope with the situation where the centre and right sensors are activated and a left turn appears appropriate. Similarly if the centre and left sensors are activated a right turn would appear to be the correct decision.

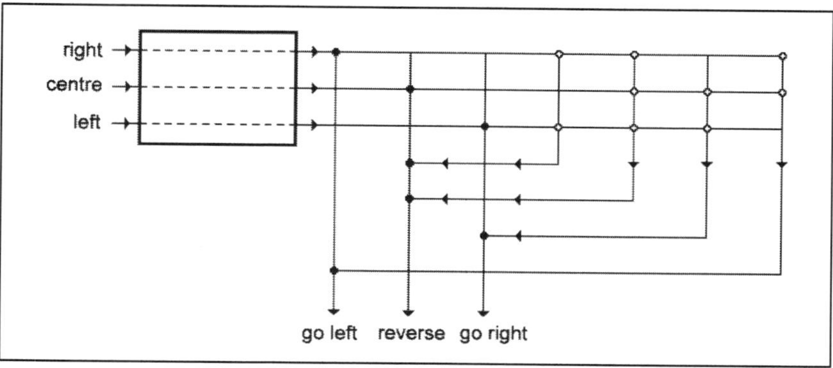

Figure 5.08

It is not difficult to see that with hundreds of sensors the wiring diagram could rapidly become hideously complicated. Nevertheless the ideas are pretty simple and a machine that acts like our creature would not be difficult to construct in principle. In the paragraph above we used the word "decision." This is typical of what happens when you begin to think about how such creatures operate and begin to ascribe human characteristics to its activities – anthropomorphism. In fact the creature in 5.08 is purely a machine – it has no memory and no thoughts. It does not learn from experience or devise clever schemes.

The Box of Tricks

You may have wondered what happens after the creature goes into reverse when it encounters a problem ahead of it. Does it spend the rest of its life in reverse? Obviously not. In practice it needs to rapidly reverse for a couple of seconds and then swim off at maximum speed, maybe making a few turns along the way. Let's go back to the creature pictured in Figures 5.01 and 5.02 and "hard-wire" it so that if the front sensor is activated it carries out an appropriate sequence as in Figure 5.09

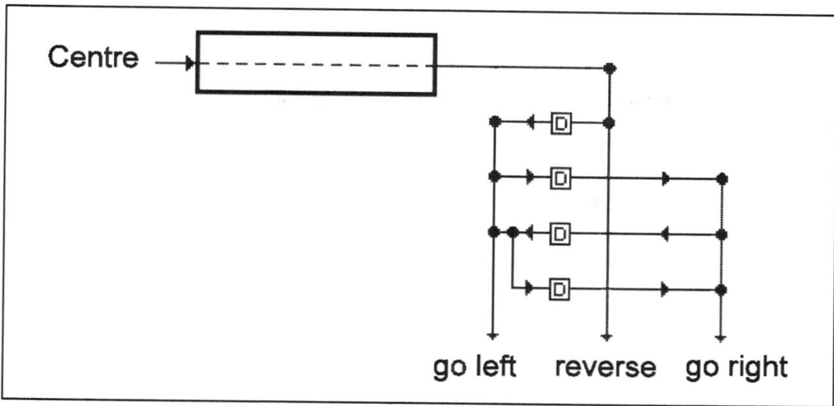

Figure 5.09

The "D" inside a square box is a delay line. If the front centre sensor is activated then it will go into reverse for a couple of seconds and then go left for a while, then right, then left and finally right again. Naturally each sensor could activate a whole sequence of actions – a touch on the right front sensor may precipitate a rapid left turn until a 180 degree turn has been achieved then a 90 degree right turn followed by an oscillating sprint.

While our creature is evolving to perform ever more complex manoeuvres its natural predators are also evolving in a classical arms race. In due course a predator will take advantage of the fact that our creature always responds in the same way to a particular stimulus. If it is to survive our creature must evolve in turn to include an element of random behaviour in its repertoire.

So far we have shown all the sensor inputs as being from external sensors but in practice there will also be signals from internal sensors – "I'm hungry"

It may be that all the signals from sight, sound, touch, smell and stomach interact in a kind of "mixing pot." One analogy we can use is with the radio set. At any given time there are thousands of radio signals around but your radio picks up just one signal. The reason it does this is that the aerial is attached to a combination of an inductor and a capacitor which resonate at a particular frequency in the same way that a tuning fork vibrates at a particular frequency. Now it would not be difficult to design a radio which lit up a series of lights to indicate what signals were present in reasonable strength. It may tell you that you can listen to any one of 25 different stations but the strongest signal by far was from your local station. You could modify the radio so that if it detected a new strong signal it sounded an alarm. Many car radios do something similar to alert you to the fact that a local station is about to give out a traffic report.

Our creature could operate in a similar fashion. There are an endless stream of signals coming in all of which are normal and expected. Suddenly a new series of signals comes in very strongly – something along the lines of "you are being eaten" Let's try to put this together in symbolic terms in Figure 5.10

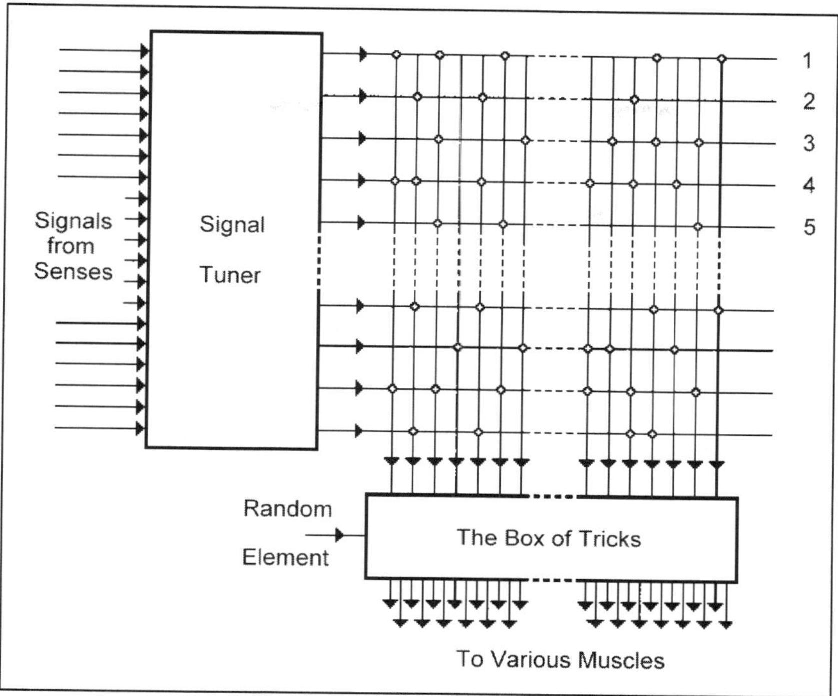

Figure 5.10

The many thousands of signals coming in from the various sense organs are tuned by the neural network into a lower number of major signals, each one of which has a significance. Lines 1, 5 and 7 lighting up may indicate that there is food ahead whereas Lines 1, 5, 7 and 29 lighting up may suggest that the food ahead is very fresh! Each of these combinations like Lines 1, 5, 7 and 29 lighting up give rise to a signal which activates the appropriate response from what we have called The Box of Tricks. This is purely mechanistic – there is no element of thought, memory or prediction. It is like when the doctor taps your knee with a hammer – your leg jerks automatically. Our creature is operating at a similar level. If food is signalled it swims forward with its mouth open and starts eating. There is no mechanism for learning new tricks but you can regard the Box of Tricks as being hard-wired Read Only memory. All of the tricks in its repertoire have evolved by chance. Those that work enable it to survive and breed in a classical evolutionary manner.

You may have noticed that the wiring diagram is beginning to look like the control lines in a digital computer. You may have also noticed that the signals coming from the "Signal Tuner" have a symbolic feel to them – Lines 1, 5 and 7 lighting up could easily be given the shorthand label "Lunch" or "Crab Fingers with mayonnaise." Also elements of feedback are creeping in. The ingredients necessary for intelligence are beginning to assemble.

I have called this a "Reactive Brain" because that is all it does – it reacts to events only. It does not remember what has happened to it personally. Nor does it plan or instigate new actions.

Chapter 6

Learning and Memory

Patient: *I'm having terrible problems with my memory*
Doctor: *How long have you had this problem?*
Patient: *What problem?*

Hard-wired Collective Memory

The brain which began to evolve in Chapter 5 was reactive – it could only react to internal ("I'm hungry") and external ("I'm being eaten") events. It had no ability to make new memories and learn from them – the memory it had was a kind of collective memory built up from hundreds of millions of years of success and failure. Ancestors who by accident made the correct decision prospered and reproduced and those that did not, did not. This is what we mean by something being hard-wired – you cannot change it without a soldering iron. Or, in the biological sense, by waiting for evolution to take its course.

Many animal reactions are driven by hard-wired memory. I can well remember seeing a dog go absolutely crazy at the sight of a green hosepipe being unrolled – presumably it evoked hard-wired memories of a snake.

Before we dismiss hard-wired memory as being for primitive creatures only, bear in mind that much of our actual behaviour, as opposed to what we tell pretty girls holding clipboards ("I would love to pay more tax to help people less fortunate than myself") is very primitive. The demand for drink, food, sex, pornography, violence, hate, envy and jealousy is enormously greater than the demand for classical music, art, physics and mathematics. Just look at the magazines at the supermarket checkout. Not many copies of the New Scientist or The History of Art there.

So, before we laugh at the dog being scared of a hosepipe, bear in mind our own hard-wired memory. I find heights pretty scary even when my rational self tells me that there is no danger. And most of us react adversely to spiders, insects and nasty smells. In each case that is for a very good reason – insect bites can kill you and nasty smells may well mean the presence of dangerous infectious agents.

This incidentally, is an appropriate moment to discuss why nice things smell nice and nasty things smell nasty. Each smell is just a complex collection of molecules and there is nothing intrinsically good or bad about it. Smell is an example of "qualia" discussed earlier. We move towards nice smells and away from nasty ones for identical reasons to the most primitive creature imaginable. The smell of freshly baked food is delicious so we move towards it. Incidentally, the fact that cooked food smells delicious must be a relatively recent phenomenon. The first cooked meal would not have had any historical reason to smell nice because it was something new with no collective memory good or bad. You could use this and the rate at which DNA changes to determine how long ago cooking was invented. If you need a PhD project there is one waiting for you.

I have a friend who is terrified by still water. He is not a wimp and worked for many years in a private coal mine – hundreds of feet underground in tunnels only 20" high digging out coal by hand. I could never see where this apparently irrational fear came from and then one day it came to me – in hot countries a stretch of still water is likely to be abounding in mosquitoes and other dangerous insects so an “irrational” desire to run away may well save your life. Very few “irrational” fears are really irrational.

As mentioned just now, I have a fear of heights but no fear of fast driving, even though the latter may be far more dangerous. Cars have only been around for a hundred years and there has been no time for a hard-wired fear of cars to arise. It has been rightly said that given enough time, people will run screaming from the sight of a condom as a fear of condoms will increase the chances of your genes being propagated. “I beg you, I beg you, do what you will with me but take off that terrible thing.” To that extent, the Catholic Church is well ahead of its time.

[Fear too is an evolutionary development, as the Donkey in Shrek summarises so eloquently. “‘Cause there’s nothing wrong with being afraid. Fear is a sensible response to an unfamiliar situation. Unfamiliar dangerous situation, I might add. With a dragon that breathes fire and eats knights, it sure doesn’t mean you’re a coward if you’re a little scared. Heeeellllppp! Shrek! Shrek! Help!”]

That’s enough sex, violence and hard-wired memory. Let’s move on to things that you remember personally. Being able to remember specific events and skills learned can be a life saver. “Valuable lessons have been learned and it is time to move on”, as UK politicians always say when they have screwed up yet again. Would this work in a court of law, I wonder? “I may have robbed a bank but valuable lessons have been learned and it is time to move on without this unhealthy preoccupation with the past.” Probably not.

It is pretty obvious why being able to remember events is useful to both humans and animals. You only need to shoot one rook and they will all disappear for months – "are you kidding – our Leonard was killed there"

Learning

As explained above, being able to record and learn from past events will greatly improve the chances of passing on your genetic material by enabling you to avoid danger and maybe know where and how to find food. Allied with the ability to communicate, it also enables a species to build up a culture and body of knowledge which can be passed on verbally to future generations ("omigod, not the lion story again"). All of which helps a group of creatures to survive and prosper. This is probably a secondary use – evolution just loves using the same facility for different purposes. Just look at the number of functions carried out by the mouth – eating, drinking, tasting, talking, gripping and breathing come immediately to mind. Even storing youngsters if you are a crocodile.

How would a very primitive creature start to learn? Well, the way to find out is to see how it could have logically evolved from what we have called hard-wired Memory. Remember that evolution can only move in an endless series of small steps. Each step must be an improvement on the previous state. It cannot take a step back in order to make progress. It cannot make a Queen sacrifice in order to achieve Checkmate. It also struggles to make big changes. That is why there is hope in the battle against HIV – for a virus to develop immunity against three different types of drug administered simultaneously is very difficult. To survive and prosper it has to make three simultaneous significant changes. If it does achieve this it will probably be as a result of somebody only bothering to take the red pills and ignoring the rest ("red is my lucky colour – I'm Pisces").

For simplicity, we will consider smell as being the most likely sense to have featured first in primitive learning. The reason for this is that from a physical and computational point of view smell is very simple and probably evolved early on. Sight and recognition are much more complex and many animals have very poor visual processing because they have never felt the need to go to all the bother of learning to see things properly (notable exceptions being creatures like the hawk where smell is not really an option).

When I say "never felt the need to" I am doing what people always do when discussing evolution – putting a result of evolution into terms that suggest motive. What I should really have said is "the species concerned has managed to prosper by using smell as its primary sense and no advantage has accrued to members of the species who have managed through chance to slightly improve their ability to see." Where people are concerned it is even easier to make this mistake. When a girl says "I'm really in love with him" when discussing her new boyfriend, she is trying to express a primitive urge in verbal form. What she really should say is "he triggers primitive physiological responses in my body that motivate me to want to conceive his children and I am powerless to resist those urges even though they may be contrary to my own best interests." But because evolution has tricked her brain she imagines that what she feels is somehow "real." Actually, dear, it's just wiring and chemicals.

Doubtless a mouse infected with toxoplasmosis tells all its friends, "I really, really want to be eaten by this cat." Take it from me, you don't. The virus has changed your brain – one of the earliest examples of a computer virus.

Back to learning. What happens is that a particular "smell" arrives as thousands of molecules drifting through the air or water – taste and smell use essentially the same mechanism. These molecules may all be absolutely identical eg that of hydrogen sulphide (the smell of rotten eggs) or a range of molecules from different chemical processes taking place in the source of the smell. They a l jostle around until they find a suitably shaped hole in the creature's smell detector to fall into. Imagine tumbling thousands of similar but oddly shaped ball bearings onto a huge table that has a special slot for every conceivable shape. Each slot has a sensor that switches on a light when it is filled. After a while a few of the slots are occupied and by looking at the lights you can see what you have caught. Remember that toy you had as a kid? It's the same principle.

Figure 6.01 A Shape Fitting Toy

Actually, of course, it is more complicated than this. For example, a new smell may well not have a specific receptor but it may sort of slot into a number of holes labelled sewage, sweet and pungent and that is how you will remember it. For convenience, you would give it a label eg "Big Scary Bird" with an odour all of its own. Bear in mind that no analogy is ever exact – otherwise it would not be an analogy but the actual truth!

If you are an expert in smell and taste you will probably start shouting that it does not work quite like that and it probably doesn't but it is close enough for our purposes. What I am trying to do is point out a possible route to the SBIE, not provide an accurate road map.

So, how would learning occur? You will have noticed from the previous chapter that this device (ie the brain of a primitive creature) has a large number of input lines from the various sensors (smell, taste, touch, sound, electric field sensing and vision) and that these go into a central point where they all interact and cross each other to then emerge as a large number of output lines to various muscles in the body. These signals all happen in real time and the basic structure does not change with time in the life of the creature.

If you absorbed nothing else you will certainly have noticed the grid like structure. In reality, these lines will not be straight, they may well be tangled like spaghetti but in a circuit diagram they would be straight. If you have ever looked inside an old valve driven radio you will see that the wires go all over the place but in a circuit diagram they are straight. Just like the famous maps of the London underground.

As mentioned earlier, even a minute change which gives a tiny, tiny advantage can be enormously powerful. One of the problems of thinking about evolution is the sheer scale of the numbers. In the case of bacteria, trillions and the time-scale, billions of years. It is a bit like thinking about the universe. You get lost in all the zeroes. So what we need is some slight change in the brain grid to introduce a smidgeon of memory. That is the thing about evolution, even a tiny, tiny advantage will put you ahead of the game over millions of years.

So far, the smell processing brain of our primitive creature looks like this.

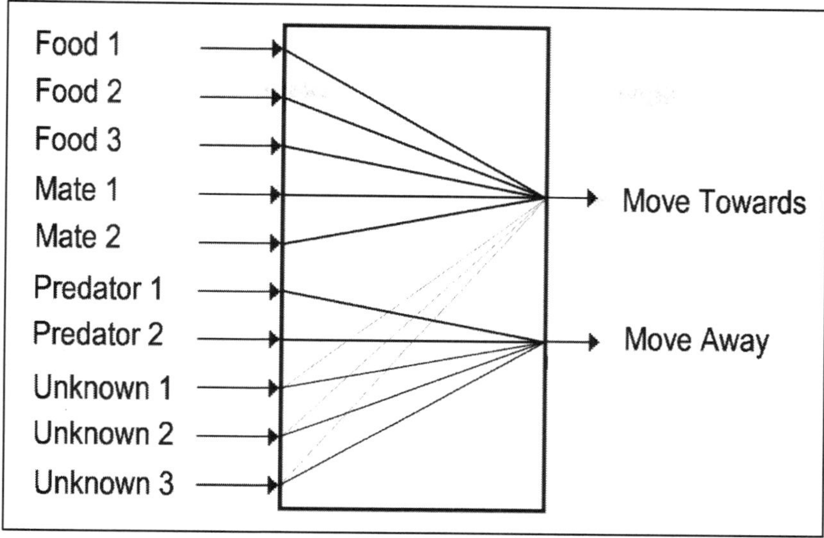

Figure 6.02 Hard-wired Reactive Memory

Bear in mind that this is still hard-wired collective memory. With no "learning memory", our creature is almost bound to move away from an unknown smell as the risk of being eaten greatly outweighs the risk of not eating. That is why the "Move Towards" links are weak and the "Move Away" links strong.

There will be certain smells that produce a very strong reaction eg food and predator. What we need is for the creature to be able to learn, for example, that a certain location, "Unknown 2" often contains food. How can this occur as a result of a minor design malfunction ie by evolution? How about this?

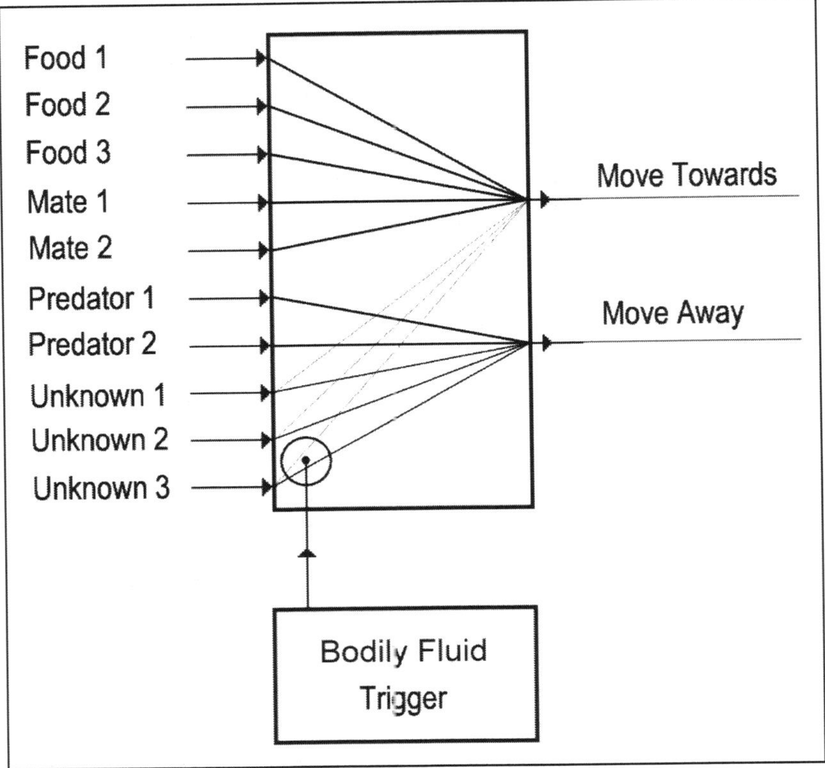

Figure 6.03 Hard-wired Reactive Memory with added Memory!

When the creature eats or hurries away from a predator, there will be some change in the composition of its bodily fluids that can be detected. The exact mechanism here does not concern us. All we are looking for is some kind of consistent change – whether you hear that a close friend is getting married by phone, text, letter or email is not relevant – what is relevant is the information, not the method of transmission.

Now the "synapses" in the brain have the magical property of being able to strengthen or weaken depending on the input they receive. This process is known as "synaptic plasticity" if you want to read more about it. Again we do not need to understand the mechanism – all we need to know is that the following can happen.

> Smell of “Unknown 3” detected → Predator then detected shortly afterwards → Adrenaline Produced → Link from “Unknown 3” to “Move Away” Strengthened

and

> Smell of “Unknown 2” detected → Food then detected shortly afterwards → Digestive Chemicals Produced → Link from “Unknown 2” to “Move Towards” Strengthened

Now, as mentioned above, this learning process may well be extremely poor, to the extent that it only helps very, very slightly. But in the Kingdom of the Blind the one eyed man is king. And in the realm of those with no memory, the one with the unbelievably bad memory is king.

Let’s imagine that a few million or maybe a few tens of millions of years have gone by and the learning ability of our creature now looks like this.

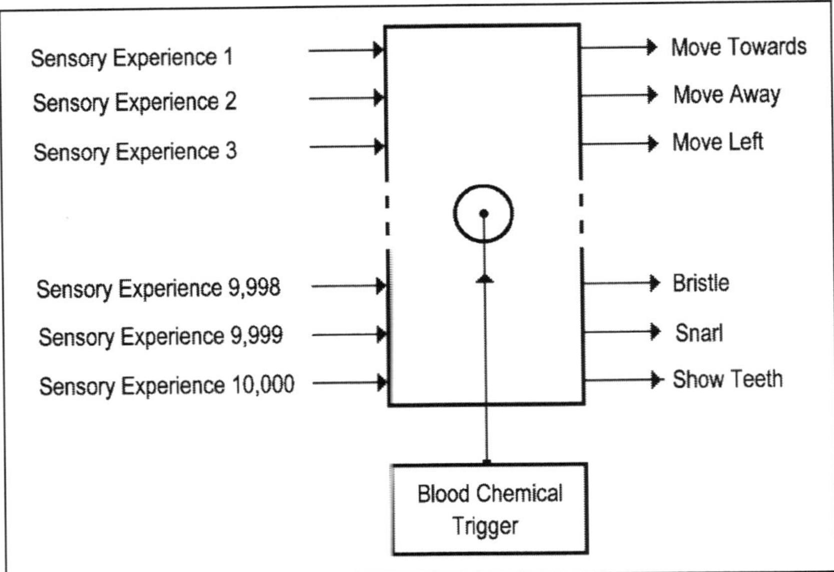

Figure 6.04 Primitive Learning

I have used the term "Sensory Experience" to include input from all the senses and it is now able to recognise a large number of such memories from its own direct experience. As before the light-bulb symbol means that the strength of synaptic connections change with events. So if this were a land based creature it would recognise the smell, roar and sight of a lion and deduce from its own memories that an appropriate response may be to do nothing if the lion is eating something or make itself scarce if the lion is clearly in hunting mode.

Although this memory is acquired from the creature's own experiences, it is similar in many ways to collective hard-wired memory. It senses something and reacts in a predictable way. There is no thought as we conceive it. It doesn't consciously think "I could stand here quietly or maybe creep away slowly." as would a human being. It just reacts with one of its many options.

What happens if its learned experience is in conflict with its collective hard-wired memory? Well, in practice it is going to react with some combination of the two. If it does a bad job then its genes are unlikely to stay around for long.

Incidentally, human beings very often have a conflict between collective hard-wired memory and decisions made in the light of experience. Is it a good idea to have sex in the stationery cupboard with the intern? Probably not if you are the President of the USA.

Real Write/Read Memory

The learning process outlined above is definitely a form of memory but a very primitive one. What we now need is a conventional memory. Consider the following typical conversation between two guys in a car.

Dave: Lookout! I don't think he saw us ...
Fred: Idiot! He could have killed us ...
Dave: Jeeze! Thank God he missed us. He must be blind not to see the stop sign
Fred: Is there a stop sign?
Dave: I can't remember but I think there is. Well, anyway if you're coming out of a side road you should stop
Fred: Do you remember that guy down the pub with the orange hair? He was killed like that
Dave: Yea but he was on a bike and probably drunk

Like the overwhelming majority of conversations, memory features prominently in this. Hard-wired, short term, long term and what I will call “look up table” memory. The latter is a term used in computing. An example. If you write a computer program to multiply together two huge numbers, namely A and B, each of say 20,000 digits, you can reduce it to a series of additions by working out the value of B x 2, B x 3, B x 4, B x 5, B x 6, B x 7, B x 8 and B x 9 and storing it in a table. This means that instead of having to work out the value of, say B x 8 some 20,000 times you do it once. This greatly speeds up the program.

So, when you see a Stop Sign on the road, you don’t start an elaborate mental process, what happens is this.

> Image reduced to its essence → Scan Lookup Table of Roadside Objects → Stop Sign

This takes such a short time that it does not even register. That is why old people are reluctant to undertake new activities because they demand a lot of mental effort. Unlike physical work it is not always obvious when you have done a lot of thinking but most of us have experienced the feeling of exhaustion when a whole series of complicated situations arise and need sorting out.

Consider this conversation when our heroes visit China.

Truk Abut Dexter

Figure 6.05 Chinese Road Sign

Dave: “Truk abut Dexter.” What the hell does that mean?
Fred: Well, I guess it means something like “Trucks are about to dexter.”
Dave: Right! So now we look out for trucks dextering ...

Fred: I got it! Dexter is Latin for right handed.
Dave: Jeeze! How the hell do you know that? You been reading stuff again? So, we're looking for right handed truck drivers.
Fred: Exactly. Watch out, that truck is turning right ...
Dave: Shit! You'd think they'd warn you.

This conversation shows heavy some weight thinking as opposed to look up table memory. But we are running ahead of ourselves. What we need is a series of small evolutionary changes that enable our dumb creature to acquire a memory that allows it to record an event and then later retrieve it. This is obviously difficult because there are two distinct processes involved here, namely writing memory and reading memory. Which came first – writing or reading? The answer must be that they evolved in tandem. Recording a memory is pointless if you cannot use it in some way.

Exactly the same logic applies to writing and reading in the conventional sense. There is not much point in writing something if nobody can read it and conversely, how can you learn to read if writing has not yet been invented? It probably started with a mark scratched on a rock meaning "there is a bear living in this cave." Or maybe saying "here there be hot chicks." Well, they do call it the world's oldest profession for a reason. And then it grew from there. This may be a fatuous example but it is a fact that many innovations in the communications field were driven by sex and pornography.

> Painting → Printing → Photography → Film → Video Recorders → The Internet → Immersion suits

and it is quite likely that early writing and drawing were similarly driven. Bear in mind that the **only** purpose of human beings is to have sex and produce more human beings. That's it. There is nothing else.

[If you are of a religious disposition, please don't bother writing to tell me that Jesus loves me and that there ***is*** *a purpose to life. I did enough sitting on hard benches being preached at as a kid to last me a life time.]*

Yet again we see the parallel between the work that evolution does and the work that humans perform using intelligence. This is a pattern that occurs again and again and is probably of profound importance. Let's call it "The Evolutionary Equivalence Hypothesis." That sounds important. Maybe we can get a grant to study it?

Here it is. "Anything that can be achieved by evolution, can in principle, be achieved by the application of sufficient intelligence." Whether this is true and if so whether it is provable, I do not know but it is another PhD project if you need one. This idea is explored further in Chapter 14.

Chapter 7

The Wiring of Human Memory

"Many a man fails as an original thinker simply because his memory is too good" Friedrich Nietzsche

In the previous two chapters we have looked at both the logic and possible wiring of a primitive brain as it evolves and acquires a memory. In this chapter I would like to look at greater length at the likely wiring and logic of personal memory in an intelligent animal such as a human being.

It must be emphasised that what I am setting out here is purely a theory of how it probably works – I have no real evidence that I am correct and it may well be that I am wrong. The following is very neat, with everything fitting into labelled boxes. In reality, these distinctions may well be not so simple and the whole lot probably looks like a spaghetti tangle. A diagram of every connection in the brain would probably cover a whole country to be legible.

[*If we made neurons at one foot interval, to give plenty of room for connections (a neuron can have as many as a thousand connections) then the plan would cover about 5,000 square miles, so not a bad guess. About the same area as Trinidad and Tobago or a bit smaller than Wales. Actually, I'm not sure that is big enough to show all the wires – there are hundreds of billions of them. You may need to build a 3 D model about 70 miles on each side ie a box with sides of 70 miles.*

You may recollect that in Chapter 3 we discovered that we needed a similar sized box to contain the universe if each star is a grain of sand. Maybe that is a total coincidence or maybe there is some deep significance in very large numbers.]

Anyway, let's look at the principles of how this could work. See fig 7.01

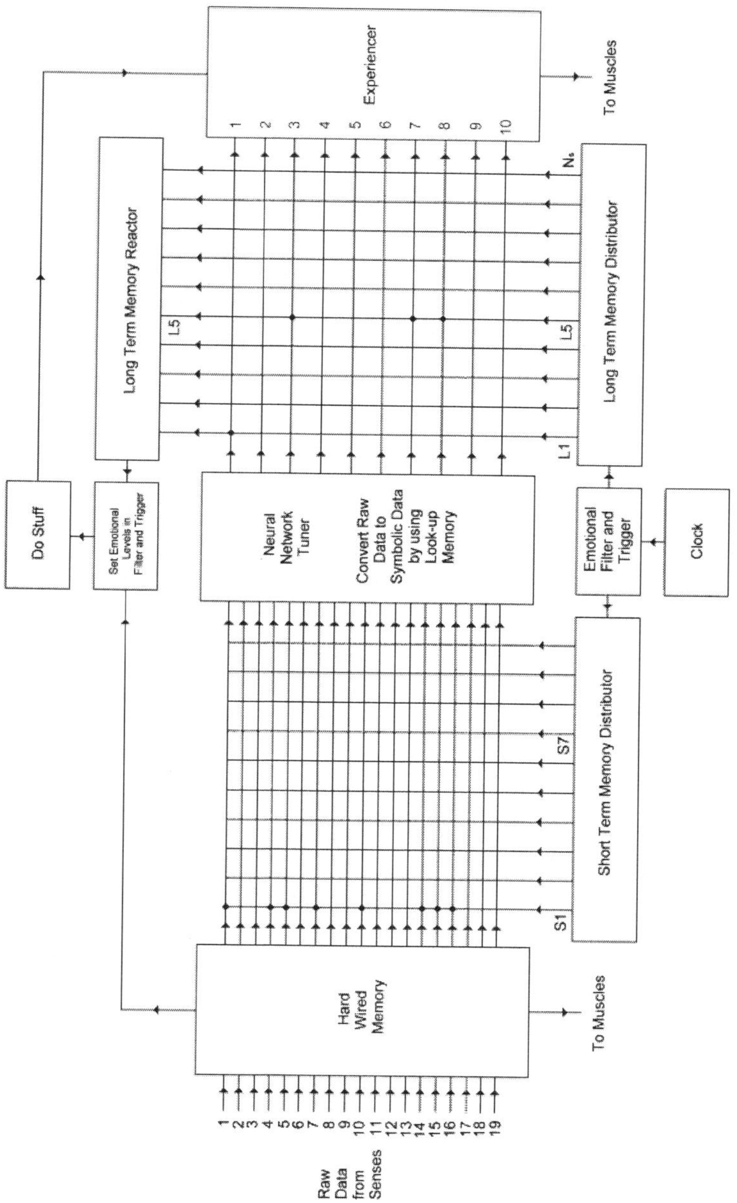
Experiencer
1
2
3
4
5
6
7
8
9
10
To Muscles
Long Term Memory Reactor
L5
Long Term Memory Distributor
L5
L1
Do Stuff
Set Emotional Levels in Filter and Trigger
Neural Network Tuner
Convert Raw Data to Symbolic Data by using Look-up Memory
Emotional Filter and Trigger
Clock
Short Term Memory Distributor
S7
S1
Hard Wired Memory
To Muscles
Raw Data from Senses
1
2
3
4
5
6
7
8
9
10
11
12
13
14
15
16
17
18
19

Figure 7.01

Component List

Clock

This is really an oscillator, as discussed in Appendix A and is directly equivalent to the clock in your PC. Not the clock that says 17.23 on Tuesday but the one that drives all of the internal electronics of memory and computation. The clock in your PC oscillates maybe three billion times per second but the human clock is more like the frequency of a cine camera – maybe 10 to 30 times per second. I would claim that the frequency of 30 times per second being like an old fashioned cine camera is no coincidence – your brain is about to start making a movie.

The clock in your PC oscillates at high frequency because it is a serial computer – in other words it does a single computation and then passes on to the next one. So, it can do 3 billion things per second in principle. The human brain, on the other hand, is massively parallel so at each clock tick, billions of things can happen to the approximately 80 billion neurons in your brain.

[Depending on design, your microprocessor may well carry out more than one operation per clock cycle. This is initially surprising but if you consider it as a sausage machine then on each cycle you could have five sausages, each one of which is skinned and drops out of a side vent. So after 6 cycles there are 30 sausages on the hopper!

Bear in mind that this is a big deal and tens of thousands of people dedicate their lives to squeezing more work out of your PC without it melting. At the same time, tens of thousands of computer programmers are writing huge inefficient programs on the assumption that the hardware will catch up later.]

Either way, both your PC and your brain can do a lot in a few seconds.

Hard-wired Memory

This has already been discussed in Chapter 6

The Tuner

This boils down to a Neural Network which recognises patterns. So you feed in a stream of raw data and it recognises it as being a plant pot or whatever. Neural Networks are discussed briefly in Appendix A. They have been a major focus of AI research and there is nothing I can add to this – any web search will show more than you want to know.

The Distributor

This is like the distributor in an old fashioned car. Or a de-multiplexer if you prefer. Whatever you call it, its job is to fire a whole row of lines one after another – a bit like the lights on an advertising sign or Christmas tree that seem to travel along.

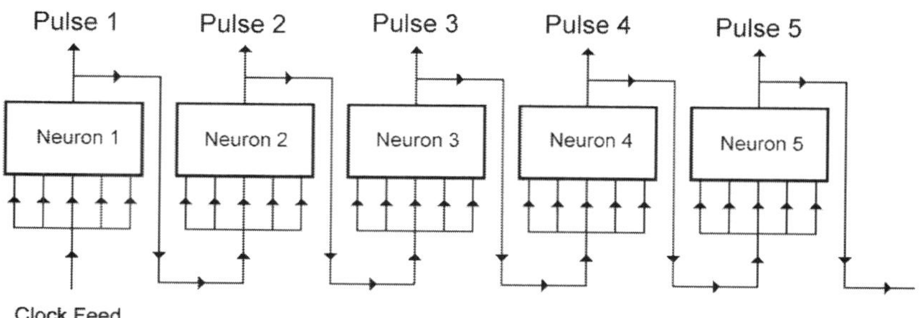

Figure 7.02 The Distributor

Where it says Neuron 1, Neuron 2 and so on these may actually be clusters of neurons but the principle is clear enough

– each neuron or cluster of neurons, causes a delay and then fires a pulse. So, when the pulse comes from the clock, it just travels along

Long Term Memory Reactor

This is yet another memory reliant black box which checks all incoming symbolic data against a list to see how it should react "boss detected → action: look busy"

The Experiencer

This is the area where you actually "experience" seeing something and is discussec at greater length in the next chapter

The Process

Look Up Memory

This is not actually shown here but is likely to be a part of normal Long Term Memory using the same principles of operation but optimised for quick access. It may take you several seconds to retrieve the face of somebody you have not seen for twenty years but you can recognise a fierce dog so quickly that you are not conscious of any delay. I mean in the general sense of "that is a fierce dog" not "that is the fierce dog belonging to the drug dealer who lives down the road next to the police station."

Short Term Memory Writing

As discussed before, reading and writing must develop together but let's look at writing first. The wiring diagram shows hard-wired memory in simplified form but in reality it will be right there in the tangle with wires going all over the place.

Let's assume that raw data arrives which your hard-wired memory interprets as a green snake. Your chemical levels and emotions change to match – your heart rate increases and adrenaline courses through your veins and you feel scared or emotionally charged, depending on which model of human you are. You may even vomit – to give a tasty meal to a predator ("yummy, I'll eat this rather than chase him") and also drop your body weight by a fraction, thereby improving your rate of acceleration. All of these are standard preparations for fight or flight.

Meanwhile the clock frequency is speeded up to a maximum of maybe 30 times per second. The "Emotional Filter and Trigger" which is "duplicated" at the top and bottom of the wiring diagram now opens to allow the clock voltage to reach the "Short Term Memory Distributor" which starts firing lines, with line S1 first. Meanwhile, we have incoming signals on lines 1, 4, 5, 7, 10, 14, 15 and 16 which signify the raw data for "green snake." Not that we know that yet – all we know is that we want to run away. The junctions of these lines are then "connected" (note the black dots) by means of synaptic plasticity (the ability of connections to strengthen or weaken) and we now "remember" the snake as raw data. The clock then fires lines S2, S3 and so on thereby starting to record the movie.

At this stage, the recording is literal and not symbolic – that is why when somebody who is talking to you suddenly says "what did I just say?" (this happens to me a lot), you have to hesitate and replay the movie for a symbolic interpretation. You can then reply "you were telling me a fascinating story about Katy's new curtains and why they don't fit properly and she is going to have to take them back to the shop"

Short Term Memory is like the RAM in your computer. And like your computer, if there is nothing for it to do, then it does nothing – there is no point in recording information that is of no importance or interest. Not that I am implying that curtains are not interesting – they are absolutely fascinating.

Writing Long Term Memory

While all of this is going on your "Tuner" is converting the raw data into "Snake" by reference to the Look Up Memory. The line L1 is lit up and a junction made with line 1. You now have a long term memory of the snake turning up. It then fires Line 2 and so on, thereby recording the "movie clip" in your brain. At the same time, all of this is playing inside your head in glorious 3-D technicolour, courtesy of the Experiencer (see next chapter)

Obviously, in reality thousands of lines (maybe even millions) are fired – the process is enormously complicated but simple in principle. One of the major reasons for long term memory being symbolic is that it uses a tiny fraction of the storage space of raw data. A photo of a green snake may use 100,000 bytes of memory but the phrase "green snake near the dustbin" uses up less than 100 bytes. The phrase "a picture is worth a thousand words" may well be true but a picture takes maybe a thousand times the memory to record it

The symbols you record are more complex than just "green snake near the dustbin." They also include a symbolic representation of the dustbin and the ground around it. These will be very approximate and this may be regarded as a fault but it is not – it is a virtue. There is no need to remember what your dustbin looks like so you don't bother. This is where we differ from autistic people who famously take a literal "photo" which stays in memory. Whereas we would just say "there was a herd of cows in the field" an autistic person may well know that there were 17 cows and be able to describe each one. This sounds impressive but in fact it represents a primitive stage of evolution.

The real achievement is to translate that into symbolic information, thereby retaining the essence of the information. Autistics tend to have trouble understanding personal relationships and are very literal. If you are a scientist or mathematician this may be an advantage but in social relationships it is not

Pupil: Miss, my pencil has broken
Teacher: Have a look in the cupboard and see if there are any pencils in there
Pupil: (goes to cupboard) Yes, there are 13 pencils in the cupboard (and returns to his desk without a pencil)
Teacher: Well, why didn't you get one then?
Pupil: Oh .. you told me to see if there were any pencils in the cupboard so that is what I did

Personal relationships are immensely complex – that is why children running round a restaurant screaming are impervious to me staring at them with hate filled eyes – they don't realise that I want to boil them in oil made from their parents' fat.

[As discussed earlier, fat is not only an evolutionary survival mechanism it is also a very handy term of abuse so it's a win, win situation.]

Once the long term memory is written the short term memory is available for further use. Long term memory is like the hard drive in your computer and is used mainly for relatively long term storage – maybe hours to years rather than seconds.

Symbolic information also makes it easier to retrieve a memory.

Reading Long Term Memory

Let us suppose that you are still in your garden wandering around when suddenly you spot something of a hexagonal shape on the ground. This time, the hard-wired memory section does not really react (apart from WTF, maybe) to the raw data coming in (your ancestors in the swamp never came across such shapes) but the Tuner translates the raw data into "red hexagon shape" and lights up all of the appropriate lines – lines 3, 7 and 8 in fact. There will be hundreds of partial matches, all of which travel up to the Long Term Memory Reactor. The LTMR then chooses the strongest signal (which corresponds to the strongest match) which happens to be in L5 (note the connecting dots), which corresponds to a child's spinning top.

[Quite how the LTMR in your brain would choose the strongest signal amongst hundreds of separate signals I am not sure but this is really just an electronics problem which any electronics undergraduate should be able to solve using a few thousand neurons.]

The LTMR in turn, then sends a pulse which resets your emotional level and triggers the clock which in turn enables the playing of a film clip of you as a child with a top that your mother (now dead) gave you for your birthday when you were 5 years old. So, you begin to remember your old mum and a feeling of great sadness sweeps over you.

How did the film clip work? Well, the rise in emotional levels meant that the Long Term Memory Distributor is now being driven by the Clock and the voltage pulse now travels in the reverse direction from that of writing memory. So, suddenly the lines leading to the Experiencer are lit up and you experience what could easily be mistaken for reality – the film clip is being read as though it were really happening. The fact that some people have difficulty distinguishing between their imagination and reality may well have physiological elements to it. In other words, their wiring is not quite right. Rather like Synesthesia but a lot less fun.

[This is enormously simplified but the key aspect is the clock firing a series of pulses that either record or recall memories like a cine film by lighting up symbolic lines where there is a good match. This is precisely how a digital computer locates memory locations. A 64 bit computer has 64 address lines. A human being probably has millions of address lines]

It is important that you realise that "really" is not really real. It is all just a magnificent illusion – all done with wires.

Straws in the Wind

As mentioned above, this is just my theory of how memory works and may well be false – perhaps it works in a totally different manner. So are there any clues that I am right? Well here are a few.

Voltage on the Brain

It is well known that a voltage probe applied to the brain may well make you see or smell something. This is consistent with my view – if you applied a voltage to the spot L5 in the wiring diagram you would see a child's top.

Layout of Wires

When I conceived this theory back in 2001 it seemed to me that it was totally at odds with most pictures of the brain but recent research (2012) shows that in fact there is an intersecting grid as I predicted. Unfortunately, I cannot show the actual picture here because of copyright reasons but the link to the original article and picture can be found by going to the MOPEKS website (mopeks.com) and clicking on 'The Book' on the navigation bar and scrolling down.

.

The Crossword Syndrome

If I say the word "cabbage" you will instantly see a picture of a cabbage but if I say something like "it is white with red and blue stripes", it will take you longer to realise that I am talking about the national flag of the UK, namely the Union Jack. That is consistent with the memory structure discussed above – it can go very quickly and simply from the word "cabbage" to a mental image and vice versa – you will immediately recognise a picture of a cabbage. But a description is much harder to grasp.

Much of human intelligence feels like a bolt on – we were not really intended to be intelligent but the advantages were so huge that it just went that way.

Chapter 8

The Experiencer

"Reality is merely an illusion" Albert Einstein

Before looking at the Experiencer in greater detail, let's look at how reality, memory and imagination are related to each other.

Reality

Well, that seems simple enough! Reality, is well, real. But of course, as with everything to do with human intelligence, it is much more complex than that. Artificial Intelligence is notorious for being a field in which people think that something is simple and then find that the closer they look, the more difficult it becomes. Interestingly, computing has some similarities. For example, when you scroll an image down a page it is pretty obvious that the image is moving down the page. Well, actually, it is not. What actually happens is as follows.

Step 1: Place the array containing the image into the memory location corresponding to the screen (the screen is a memory location)
Step 2: Is the user scrolling down? If so then continue to Step 3
Step 3: Build a new array representing the current location
Step 4: Return to Step 1

So really it is like a movie. A series of separate images creating the illusion of movement. Similarly, when you click a button with your mouse and it depresses that is also an illusion – it would be simple to make a button that always did the exact opposite of what you expect or indeed something totally random and bizarre. Hence the nerdy joke. "It's not a fault – it's a feature"

The brain seems to have a whole repertoire of tricks to make you think(!) that what you are experiencing is real. I recall watching a TV programme where a man explained that he had had an accident that damaged his nose with the result that he experienced a dreadful smell all the time. He further explained that to avoid embarrassment, he spent a fortune on air fresheners so that other people would not smell it. Yes, really.

Back to what passes for reality. So how does it work? If you re-examine Fig 7.01 in Chapter 7, you will see that I have shown the Experiencer as being fed with symbolic rather than raw data. There are a number of reasons to suppose this is the case.

Firstly, it is well known that the eye has a blind spot (because the optic nerve is in the wrong place) and yet when you look at something there is no "black hole" – clearly the brain is filling in the missing details. Magicians use this fact to fool you. And drivers quite often hit things that are not there.

Secondly, when we see colours, this is a false representation as all we can really sense is different frequencies of light. So what you actually "see" is a synthetic model of reality. That is why, even if you have seen a rug on the floor for months you may still have no idea what it looks like unless you look at it directly and absorb that information. The brain clearly works like a security service – on the "need to know" basis. For everyday matters, you have no need to know what the rug looks like so your brain does not waste time on storing the information – it is like those wonderful old maps "here there be dragons." Or, this case, "here there be a rug." What kind of rug you have no idea. Unless you are especially interested in rugs, of course.

So, reality as we experience it, is an illusion – a kind of PR fantasy.

Memory and Imagination

It seems to me that Memory and Imagination are poles apart. At the one extreme you have the person with a very bad memory but a brilliant imagination who can cope with complex social situations and at the other extreme the autistic who can take a mental photograph of a herd of cows in a field and then later count and describe them but has difficulty understanding and coping with social situations which most of us do not even realise are complex.

In the brilliant (and well researched) film, "My name is Khan", in which Shahrukh Khan plays the part of a young man with Asperger Syndrome, there is a wonderful dinner party where the conversation goes something like this.

Host: Would you care for a little dinner?
Khan: No. I would like a lot of dinner

Later ...

Host: How is your dinner?
Khan: It is not very good.

Incidentally, this film covers a whole host of controversial subjects in an original manner and is well worth seeing – unlike most Indian films which are pretty dreadful. The other great exception, also starring Shahrukh Khan, is “Om Shanti Om”, which is a work of towering genius. And with hot chicks too. Thousands of ’em to quote Michael Caine yet again.

Or how about “Thank you. We’re all refreshed and challenged by your unique point of view.” That last comment was picked up from the web and appears to have been repeated about half a million times. Yes, bitchy comments are a very popular art form – infinitely more popular than poetry. Part of the appeal is that their true meaning is diametrically opposed to their apparent meaning. When we build a SBIE that can make and understand such malicious put-downs, we have really cracked it. “I enjoy working with people – it reminds me of how far I have come.”

Obviously, the role of imagination does not only relate to social relationships but they probably represent the most difficult problem that evolution has had to cope with. Our ability to understand the actions and motives of other people is probably one of evolution’s finest achievements. One on which we place very little value.

Memory Playback

Earlier, I have referred to the playing back of a memory as being like the playing back of a film clip. That is a simplification. If you are ever the cause of a car crash you should round up as many witnesses as possible – in court your lawyer will tear them to shreds as they stumble and contradict themselves, never mind each other. “But you just said it was the red car coming from the left that hit the green car coming from the right but now you are saying it was the red car turning right that hit the green car turning left.”

The reality is that if all the witnesses agree with each other then they have been coached and are lying. One of the signs of being a spy is that you always repeat the cover story perfectly. In reality, memory is not like that. Rather than being a film clip it is really a series of descriptions, which your brain then turns into a mental "picture"

Clip 1: I am driving south down Portland Street and have just stopped for a red light at the junction with Princess Street.
Clip 2: A green car comes past me and sails through the red light
Clip 3: A black taxi and a brown car start moving forward from the right as their light turns green
Clip 4: The green car ploughs into the taxi and the brown car and several other cars also collide
Clip 5: The taxi is now facing backwards but is only dented on its right which seems impossible
Clip 6: Everybody stops in amazement

Every time I replay this in my head it looks a little different but it definitely happened and I was there.

Imagination and Innovation

Imagination seems to have two similar but different meanings in everyday usage. Consider the following.

1: Imagine a wooden bowl of fruit containing two oranges and three apples
2: Imagine how you would escape from a sinking ship

For that reason, I have used the word "innovation" to describe the process involved in the second example.

The Experiencer Itself

You can imagine it as a black box which receives symbolic information from a number of possible sources and turns it into a 3 D "picture" in your head. This, as mentioned before, is the greatest qualia of them all. Those colours are not real – they are just frequencies. And those roses do not really smell nice – they just trigger a voltage pulse on one of the lines. And the 3-D is just a glorious illusion brought about by having two eyes. Unless, you were born totally blind, in which case it will produce a mental "picture" featuring only sound, touch and smell.

There are at least four circumstances where the "viewing" of symbolic information is involved.

1: Reality
2: Memory recall
3: Imagining a static or dynamic scene
4: Conceiving an innovative process

Whether these are all actually viewed in the same "black box" or similar black boxes is not that material. As already mentioned, evolution just loves using the same thing for different purposes but it also is good at building duplicate copies – your left arm did not evolve separately from your right arm.

The actual "experience" may well be an emergent property of the brain – like consciousness. Fortunately we do not need to actually comprehend how it works. The ability to be able to experience reality, memories and new ideas is of course, of central importance to understanding how the brain works. Or is it? The more I try to tie this down, the more elusive it becomes.

As explained later, the fact that it is hard to comprehend does not really matter – what matters ultimately in our quest to build a Silicon Based Intelligent Entity ('SBIE') is whether we can write computer code to emulate it. My conclusion is that right at the heart of the Experiencer is an incredibly flexible 3-D model which is really just a mathematical simulation of versions of reality. In animals, this model deals with real objects in real environments but in humans it can also deal with intangible objects in imaginary environments.

For simplicity, we will call this model The Simulator and it features in Chapter 10. Just after we deal with human problem solving.

An Experiment

Here is an interesting experiment.

Place a person in a darkened room and move an illuminated white disk slowly towards them and check which lines are activated in the brain. If I am right, there should be considerable activity in the lines leading directly from the eye but much more interesting and significant activity elsewhere which would give a clue to the actual symbolic aspects of processing.

The latter activity may be too small to notice but as the disk is moved or replaced by say a picture of a house, it should become more noticeable.

Chapter 9

Human Problem Solving

"The essence of solving a problem is to formulate it"
Albert Einstein (loose translation)

It is my belief that human beings solve problems in the following manner.

1. The Identification of the relevant environment eg "In my garden" and the relevant objects in that environment eg "me, pond, frog." These objects may well be of an abstract nature in a complex environment eg "justice" in the environment of "the law."

It is arguable that it is sufficient to be able to identify just the relevant objects and their characteristics as the environment is then implicit but this may not always be true.

2. A Memory that can store and retrieve the properties and possible actions ('Methods') of those objects eg "green alligator" and "alligator snaps."

3. A Memory that can store and retrieve events involving those objects eg "Last Saturday, Mrs Jones who lives next door, said she had an alligator in her pool"

4. The generation and use of "Procedures" which are a series of actions carried out by objects using their methods eg "I leaned down to look at the frog in the pond and then my phone fell into the water and when I tried to catch it, I fell in too." The

generation of procedures, is directly equivalent to a computer program that is able to generate computer programs which in turn can use each other.

5. A Simulator that can model and run any conceivable procedure in any conceivable environment eg "To escape the big dog in the park, I will climb this tree." The creation of a model that mirrors how something works and has predictive powers is what we call "comprehension" or "understanding"

If you have used the computer program MOPEKS you will have noticed that it incorporates most of these features (with the exception of memory of events). I hope to show that MOPEKS is the route to real intelligence.

Let's suppose you are sitting in a chair in your garden reading the newspaper and things begin to happen. Let's see how these events relate to Figure 9.01 which follows.

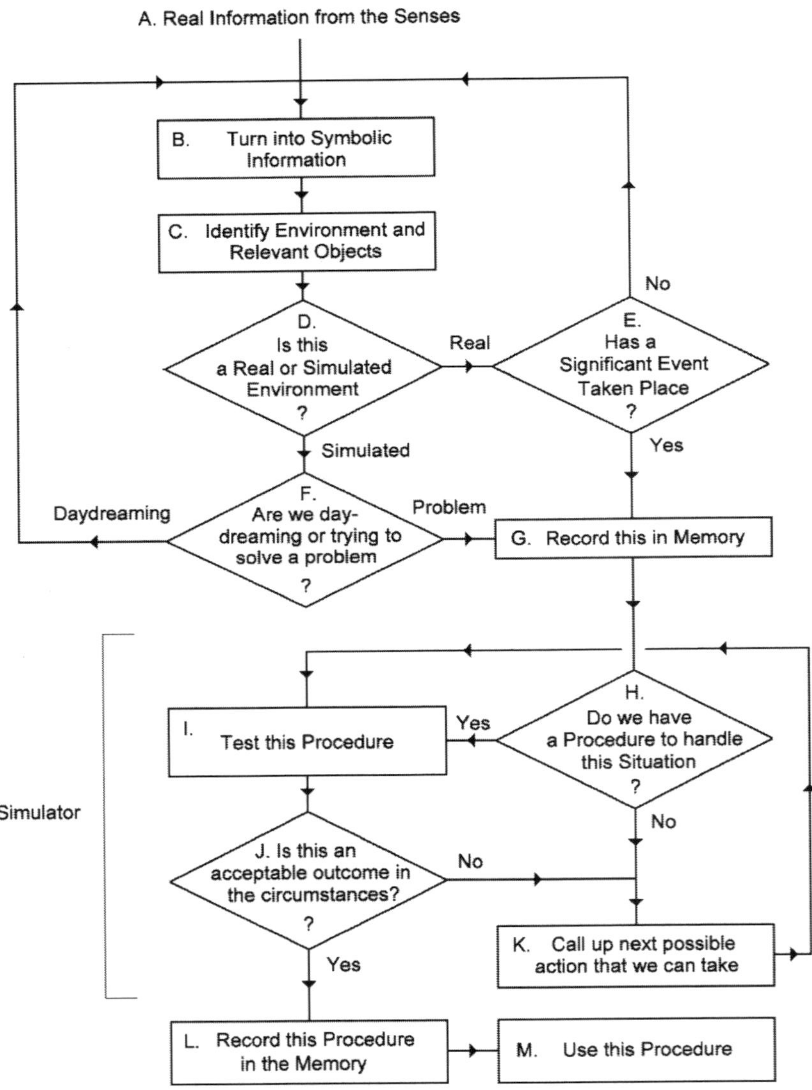

Figure 9.01 Human Problem Solving

A. Real Information from the Senses

In a human being this information is pretty obvious – vision, hearing, smell, taste and touch. Vision, hearing and smell are in stereo (that is why we have two nostrils) and the rest is in mono. It all arrives as a series of electrical signals at the brain.

B. Turn into Symbolic Information

The flow of information from the senses is vast but mostly irrelevant. It needs to be transformed into something much simpler, as discussed previously. In this case, "sitting in a chair reading a newspaper in my garden."

C. Identify the Environment and Relevant Objects

It is possible that your brain firstly identifies the objects then the environment or maybe the other way round or maybe in an iterative manner. Whatever the route, in this case your brain will identify your environment as "a chair in my garden." The relevant Objects are initially anything and everything you can see eg a tree, a pond, a stick etc

D. Is this a Real or Simulated Environment?

If you are actually sitting in a chair in your garden then your environment is real. If, on the other hand, like now, you are imagining it, then the environment is simulated. This is very important.

Level 1 Intelligence – A Real Environment

What I have called here "Level 1 Intelligence" concerns a real creature reacting to real events as they happen. A fox in a field trying to catch a raven is using “Level 1 Intelligence.” So, I am going to ask you to really take a chair and a newspaper out into your garden. Right, so you are now actually there with the newspaper? No cheating! Are you sitting comfortably? Then I’ll begin ...

“Nothing much happening here but my brain will keep monitoring the signals coming in from my senses. I guess I have been here an hour or so now. Omigod! What is that? It is sort of brown and slithery looking. And I am sure I heard a noise ...

E. Has a Significant Event Taken Place? Yes!

Too damn right! My pulse rate has shot right up. It looks like a rattlesnake ...

G. Record this in Memory!

No chance I will forget this. But what was I doing this time yesterday? I have no idea, so clearly it was not important and my brain did not bother to record it as a significant event.

I. Do I have a Procedure to handle this? No!

In other words, is finding a rattlesnake in my garden something that I have either experienced or given careful thought to? No, it is not! So what can I do? Well, what I do is go through a list of all the things that are possible in this environment.

Carry on reading
Stand up carefully
Yell
Smile
Grin

Scratch my ear
Pray
Walk away
Undo my shirt
Comb my hair
Play a recording of something from my mobile phone
Fall off the chair
Take a photograph
Call the Police
Check Facebook

This list probably extends to a hundred or so conceivable actions I can take but taken in combination there are tens of thousands of possible procedures. So, I try out a selection of procedures in the Simulator (see next chapter). It is my contention that this is what we know as "Innovation." The trying out of new procedures in unexpected ways

H & J. Test this Procedure and Is this an Acceptable Outcome in the Circumstances?

This is a new Procedure that my brain is testing, "wet my pants and then fall off the chair." The simulator tests this but finds that the outcome is not that good. So it, tests the next possibility "stand up and walk towards the snake and hold out my hand." That is even worse. It evaluates some thousands of possible procedures in maybe two or three seconds. It may be that many of these "evaluations" are cursory or amount to instant rejection but this is just an optimising feature of the simulator and does not affect the principle of what happens.

I am not consciously aware of this any more than I am consciously aware of 99% of the things that my body does. I do not need to be aware. All I need to be aware of is that my brain is evaluating possible procedures. Ah! It has found a pretty good outcome. "keep perfectly still and then inch away very, very slowly. When I am a fair distance away, run"

L & M Record this Procedure in my Memory and then Use this Procedure

"So I kept perfectly still and then inched away very, very slowly and then ran to the house. Actually, it wasn't a snake – it was some bark fallen off a tree and the noise I heard was my newspaper rustling. But I still remember it to this day!"

Level 2 Intelligence – A Simulated Environment

Now in the example above you were actually sitting in your garden reading a newspaper. It really happened. This time rather than actually doing it, I want you to imagine doing it. This is a lot more difficult to do but I think you will manage it. Because you're are a human being and have the circuitry to make it possible. Otherwise you would not be reading this.

A. Real Information from the Senses

"As before there is real information coming in but this time it is words from this book. But I am aware that people are moving around and that my boss is still at lunch ..."

B. Turn into Symbolic Information

"I am sitting at my desk in the office reading a book which has asked me to imagine that I am sitting in my garden reading a newspaper."

C. Identify the Environment and Relevant Objects

"My primary environment is the office but I am now going to imagine sitting in a chair in my garden reading a newspaper. So the environment that is relevant is 'in a chair in my garden'. Just like it was when it really happened."

F. Are we Daydreaming or trying to Solve a problem?

Sometimes we daydream just to enjoy the sensations that result but let's not go there right now (see later). In this case we have a problem to solve.

The rest of what follows is identical to what happens when you did this for real. You can see how easy it is to confuse reality with imagination. When you hear somebody recount an event that you observed, you will know how they re-write the story to make it seem more interesting. And as the years roll by, it gets better and better until it becomes a piece of pure fiction that they believe happened. Don't worry – I do that too.

Level 3 Intelligence – A Simulated Environment in a Simulated Environment

"I am driving my car while imagining sitting in my office while I read a book which asks me to visualise sitting in a chair in my garden reading a newspaper." Obviously, this could go on forever. In practical terms, I would guess that it is rarely necessary to go much beyond Level 3, although, in reading and understanding the above you are operating at Level 4. But it is a strain.

Level N Intelligence – Dreaming

It is possible that dreams have no purpose but this seems unlikely – animals which have useful dreams would soon outpace and replace animals that do not. Now "useful" could include "entertaining" – so the ability to have fun dreams may put you ahead of the game. Maybe just by impressing girls. The ability to entertain an audience has definite evolutionary advantages – the phrase "singing for his supper" arose for a reason in a society where food is extremely valuable. To us, being without food means that maybe you can fit into your favourite pair of jeans. For much of history being without food meant death – not to mention the flies and stuff.

Or perhaps the existence of dreams gave a pretext for outright lying. "I had a dream where you came and lived with me and I discovered a vast cave full of treasure and you became queen of the tribe." Yea, sure you did. You may laugh at such obvious deceit but throughout history the dreams (or lies) of priests and other charlatans have assumed great significance. "If you cross the river, a great empire will be destroyed." Right! But you forgot to say which one – theirs – or mine? Oops! It was mine ...

But behind all this flim-flam, it seems to me that dreaming is probably a continuation of problem solving as discussed above but with the constraints and optimising procedures removed. If you are awake and need a solution to a problem, you only evaluate possibilities which are, er, possible. That is because you often need a solution right now and do not have time to explore the realms of the very unlikely or impossible. That seems to be built in – if you need to escape from a mad dog, you don't start evaluating solutions which involve eating rice pudding but in a dream you may well do just that. In a dream, you have plenty of time (maybe all night) and you can drift off into fantasy and construct whole edifices which are ridiculous but may just give a clue to something real and profound. “I was riding on a rocket ship at close to the speed of light and ... hang on a minute, where’s my pen, Mileva?”

As always, you need to distinguish between what you are aware of (the dream, in this case) and the vast amount of processing going on inside your brain. What you see as your dream is really just a PR release. In Chapter 3, I mentioned that you can solve real life problems by “instructing” your brain to work on the problem overnight – much of MOPEKS was built that way. I think that if you just go to sleep without having given your brain its overnight processing load, it will just freelance and explore almost random chains of “logic.” And maybe come up with something useful – or maybe not.

The **daydream** is somewhere between real life and dreaming and involves, yet again, the suspension of constraints. It is not normally an attempt to solve a problem but just an attempt to create illusions of success in some particular objective – often something that you would not wish to see on the front pages. I remember seeing a cartoon where a couple both drop a coin into a wishing well. In the next frame they are both falling down the well. Enough said.

Does this Model Always Work in Solving Problems?

There may be situations where this methodology does not cope, even in principle but I have not found one yet. Of course, being able to set out how a process works is not the same thing as being able to implement it, but it is a start. For example, the following model of the brain is guaranteed to do everything that a human brain can do.

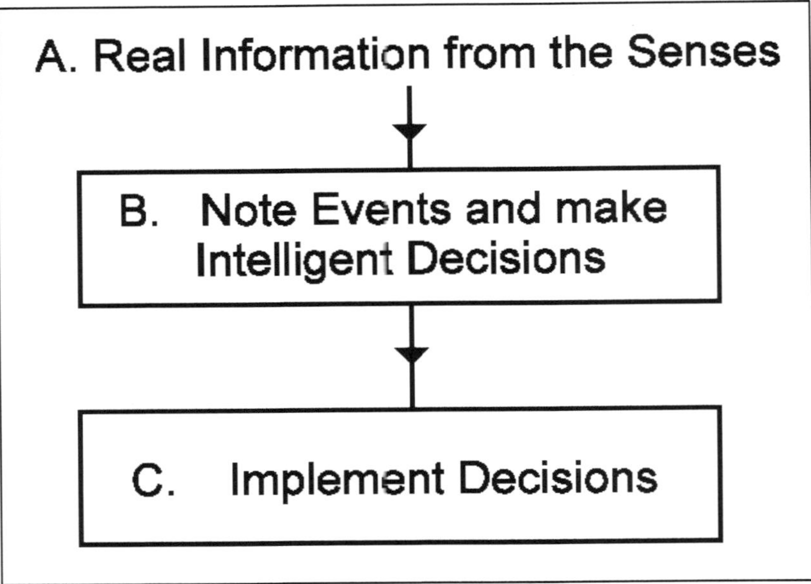

Figure 9.02 All Encompassing but Useless

Not a lot of use, though is it! So, can we make it work in silicon and computer code?

Chapter 10

The Simulator

"A mind is a simulation that simulates itself" Erol Ozan

In the last chapter we looked at the logic of Human Problem Solving which centred around the Simulator. But what about the actual wiring? How does the brain actually do all this stuff? Well, what follows is my best guess. Maybe I am right in which case cheers all round. If I am wrong, then maybe others can improve on it.

Either way much scientific and engineering progress is based on people making guesses – or "formulating hypotheses" if you prefer it. These are then discarded, modified or adopted. In the latter case they then become "respectable" and are then presented as if they were arrived at by logical processes instead of guesswork. That is because guesswork does not really sound very scientific.

Interestingly, a similar process happens in computing. In theory you write a specification and then you write a computer program that follows the specification. In practice, you start writing some code to see whether the key ideas work. When you get something working you then write some of the specification to reflect your experience so far and then you write some more code and so on. This process has now been made respectable by the appellation "Agile Development" as well as a whole host of similar names.

A Primitive Simulator

In Chapter 7 we built a model of how personal memory (as opposed to hard-wired group memory) may well work. This was illustrated in Fig 7.01. Now, as mentioned many times before evolution normally moves in tiny incremental steps. I say normally because big steps may occur but take much longer.

So how could that memory model change into something which can solve problems in a primitive manner? Well, Fig 10.01 below is identical to the personal memory illustrated in Fig 7.01. The only change is at the bottom right hand side where I have added another black box.

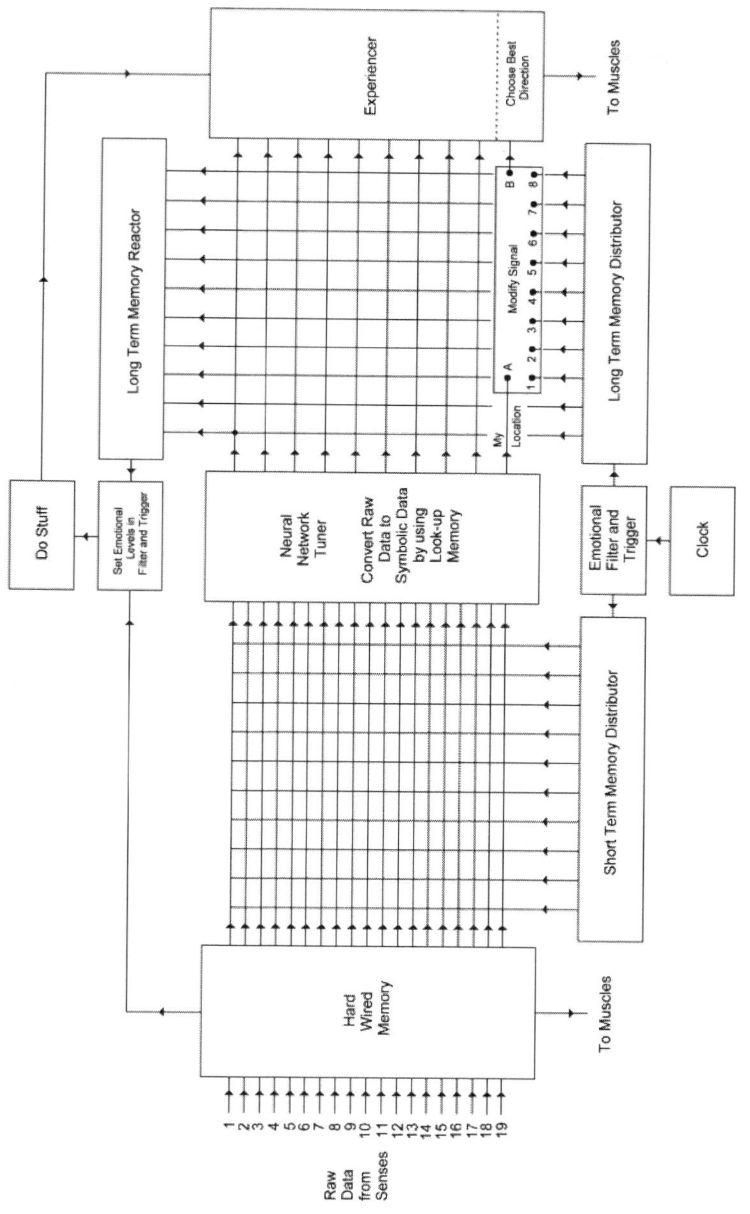

Experiencer
Choose Best Direction
To Muscles
Long Term Memory Reactor
Modify Signal
A
B
1
2
3
4
5
6
7
8
My Location
Long Term Memory Distributor
Do Stuff
Set Emotional Levels in Filter and Trigger
Neural Network Tuner
Convert Raw Data to Symbolic Data by using Look-up Memory
Emotional Filter and Trigger
Clock
Short Term Memory Distributor
Hard Wired Memory
To Muscles
1
2
3
4
5
6
7
8
9
10
11
12
13
14
15
16
17
18
19
Raw Data from Senses

Figure 10.01

Suppose the bottom signal emerging from the Neural Network Tuner represents my location. Normally this is just part of the information pack that is delivered up to the Experiencer to "experience" what is going on and react. But now it is processed by a black box which in turn is driven by the Long Term Memory Distributor so that the way is open for a number of alternatives to be evaluated. In the layout I have shown 8 but there may be dozens. Each time one of these alternatives is lit up, the Long Term Memory Reactor changes the Emotional setting.

So, if it did evaluate 8 possible nearby locations, the one which causes the least "fear" may well be to head to my right. So that is what I do. I have evaluated a number of possible courses of action and chosen one of them.

Note that, yet again, evolution is using something (the Long Term Memory Distributor in this case) for a use different to that for which it originally evolved.

Clearly, this is very primitive but you can see that the model is moving towards a brain which can evaluate different alternatives and choose the most attractive.

Like wow – I'm thinking!

An Advanced Simulator

The Primitive Simulator above only looks ahead by one step and does not anticipate the actions of other participants – principally that of predator or potential meal. This is an excuse for one of my favourite quotes.

"I know you probably hear this all the time from your food, but you must use bleach or something 'cause that's one dazzling smile you got there!" Donkey to the Dragon in Shrek

So, how would you evaluate the possible result of many possible steps from many other participants? To do that you need to have a record of the properties and possible actions of these other participants. That is precisely what MOPEKS does. It then places all of these objects in a generalised simulator and tries out various strategies.

In this particular case, the computer model has run ahead of the reality on which it is based. In other words, I built MOPEKS without having worked out exactly how the human brain carries out such steps.

Chapter 11

MOPEKS® the Program

"The question of whether computers can think is like the question of whether submarines can swim" Edsger W. Dijkstra

Introduction

This chapter is duplicated on the MOPEKS website, (mopeks.com) and appears, via the navigation bar, as 'Guide → How it Works'. The version on the website is likely to be more up to date and should be read instead of this chapter if practicable.

If you wish to know how to actually **use** MOPEKS you should read the rest of the website and download a copy of MOPEKS to experiment with. Please also note that this chapter is to some extent a summary of this book so there are elements of repetition.

MOPEKS is a Registered Trademark and stands for Methods, Objects, Properties, Environments, Kinetics and Simulation. The blue logo is also a Registered Trademark. Certain aspects of MOPEKS are the subject of patent applications in all of the major countries in the world.

Private individuals and non-commercial organisations are welcome to use MOPEKS freely and develop the principles, provided that due acknowledgement is given to MOPEKS as the source of such work.

Commercial organisations need to be aware that I have the means, determination and experience to defend my interests. To quote the Wright brothers "we did not do this to make money but if anybody is going to make money, it should be us." If you **are** a commercial organisation and you wish to use these principles please contact me via the 'Contact' page on the website to discuss the best way forward.

This project began in 1986 when I read the classic book by Douglas Hofstadter, **Gödel, Escher, Bach: An Eternal Golden Braid.** This started a 27 year obsession with the nature of intelligence and whether it would be possible to firstly understand how human intelligence works and secondly build a computer program that showed a possible route to a Silicon Based Intelligent Entity ('SBIE').

This Book, the program MOPEKS and The Website www.mopeks.org are the result.

Understanding the Human Brain

I have read many books which purport to explain how the human brain works but invariably they seem to boil down to a description of what it does, which is not quite the same thing. There are no circuit diagrams or logic flowcharts showing how you could start to build one. They are descriptions of the classic blackbox – we don't know what is inside or how it works but this is how it behaves.

It is my belief that there is no magic or mystery here – it is a meat computer that takes input, evaluates it and then updates its memory and makes intelligent decisions when required. For many centuries the debate was complicated by the nature of the human soul but that is no longer something that concerns the majority of people who are looking at this problem.

Some of the modern stumbling blocks are such things as consciousness and the nature of comprehension. These are all fascinating subjects but in my opinion are irrelevant. This is an engineering problem – all we want is a computer program that emulates human intelligence. Whether it is really conscious or really intelligent as opposed to "pretending" to be need not concern us. What matters is whether it can get a job in a call centre selling double glazing.

Of course, the biggest stumbling block of all seems to be that nobody appears to know how it works. But it is a machine and as such must operate on logical principles.

I have tackled the problem by trying to understand how it must have evolved. Evolution is the driving force and the first creatures to exhibit the ability to respond to events may well have been quite simple. Subsequent versions will have shown steady improvement with the occasional great leap forward.

The Holy Grail(s)

The evolution of human designed computers has gone through the following phases.

Phase 1 – mechanical analogue computers. The simplest example being the slide rule. Actually, it is arguable that an ordinary measuring rod is an analogue computer but that is really just semantics.

Phase 2 – purely mechanical digital computing devices, of which Babbage's Difference Engine No.2 is the most celebrated example. This was designed specifically to carry out simple mathematical calculations.

Phase 3 – electrical analogue computing devices such as gun-fire control systems on battleships.

Phase 4 – electro-mechanical digital computing devices which can only solve a particular problem, eg 'Bombes' used to decode secret messages at Bletchley Park. In order to carry out a different task you need to take out your tool kit and start moving things around physically.

Phase 5 – programmable digital computers like your PC. These can in principle solve any problem for which a logical route can be specified. To do so they require a specific program written by a human programmer. This program is then run on the computer and carries out a particular task which may be general in the sense that it can cope with a variety of different types of input but invariably of a particular class of problem.

It is **never** necessary for the user of the program to modify the hardware.

Phase 6 – a computer program that can write useful computer programs with a minimum of instruction – this is the "Holy Grail of Computing" which will make millions of human computer programmers redundant.

The "Holy Grail of Artificial Intelligence" is a computer program that passes the Turing test and is therefore considered to be genuinely intelligent.

It is arguable that both of these goals amount to the same thing in practice. You send it an email asking it to write a program which could win at online poker, say. It would then ask you a few general kinds of questions and then in a few days (or hours or even minutes) send back the program and a set of operating instructions.

I believe that MOPEKS represents a start on Phase 6 insofar as its output is computer programs which can use each other in an ever-ascending evolutionary ascent to solve real life problems.

MOPEKS® – the Philosophy

MOPEKS uses the principle of Genetic Programming (see Appendix B) to generate simple computer programs. There is nothing especially innovative about this – GP has been around for about 30 years.

Where I believe MOPEKS is genuinely innovative is that it is able to take this process much further. Each useful program that is generated can be placed in a library and used in turn to create other computer programs.

MOPEKS also allows the user to construct arbitrary Environments in which a number of arbitrary Objects can operate. These Objects also have arbitrary Properties which can be decided by the user. For example, the environment might be a table top on which various objects compete for space. These computer programs (called "Methods") can also be attached to objects to enable one of the objects to solve a specific problem.

For example.

One of the objects in the solar system may be a space ship and the problem is to reach another planet by using the sling-shot gravitational effect

or

There may be a man out on the veldt pursued by a dangerous animal and his objective is to kill it by luring it into quicksand

or

A man may need to visit a number of cities with the minimum amount of travelling (the "Travelling Salesman" problem)

In principle, therefore, MOPEKS is a general purpose problem solver modelled on human intelligence.

MOPEKS® – Program Organisation

The parts of MOPEKS which are not time critical are written in Visual Basic 6. The time critical parts are written in a mixture of Visual C++ 6 and Assembler. Most of the bit manipulation is also carried out in Assembler.

I am aware that Visual Basic 6 is now obsolete but when I started this quest it had not even been released. Much of the early work was written in QB4.5 and Quick C. In due course it may be appropriate to change over to .net

Ironically for a program that generates Objects, Methods and Properties, MOPEKS has not been coded as an Object Oriented Program.

Every aspect of MOPEKS was conceived and written by me

personally and no other parties were involved in this venture. Having said that, I have received a lot of assistance from the usual sources on the technical aspects of programming. For example, if I needed to know how to generate pseudo random numbers or access the Microsoft Cryptography Key I would look on the web or ask on a forum. All computer programs contain components written by others and MOPEKS is no exception. Thank you everybody.

It may be that at some stage the source code will be released as “open source” (but not yet) in which case other people may wish to port the code to .net and make it object oriented.

The program naturally breaks down into a number of sections which have been named after the areas of a commercial organisation, namely Stores, Workshop, Factory-Simulator, Quality Control, Darkroom, Laboratory, Library, Line Library and Office. Like all analogies, this is merely illustrative of the functions which can be carried out in the separate sections and is for ease of reference only.

The role of these various sections is explained at greater length here in due course.

In Object Oriented Programming (‘OOP’) a Method is something that carries out a series of actions. In a language such as Visual Basic it would be called a function or a subroutine.

In MOPEKS, I have used the term ‘Method’ to describe a computer program which is derived from raw data by the ‘Factory’ and the ‘Simulator’. The derived Method should then be able to reproduce all (or the relevant part) of that data and also reproduce the actions of whatever produced that data.

So, for example, if the data represents the distance between two particular objects in a series of trials, then the derived Method should **always** be able to compute the distance between **any** two objects.

Similarly, a Method derived from data showing the progress of an object as it pursues another object, should be able to predict the position of **any** object which is pursuing another object.

You can view such a Method as a generalised explanation of an observed phenomenon.

Q. 'Can you understand why the sun rises in the east and sets in the west?'
A. 'Here is a derived Method that reproduces that behaviour'

Q. 'What is this series of numbers?'
A. 'Here is a derived Method that reproduces each number **and the rest of the series too**'

Such derived Methods are at the heart of MOPEKS. Here is a Method generated by MOPEKS that finds the square root of a number.

```
Private Function SquareRoots(ByVal R As Double) As Double
    'Problem Description: '01Square Roots'
    'Generated by MOPEKS at 1.01 pm on Friday 12th April 2013

    Dim ax As Double, bx As Double, cx As Double, dx As Double

    1: ax = R + 1
    2: bx = R / ax
```

```
    3: ax = bx + ax
    4: ax = ax / 2
    5: If bx < R / ax Then GoTo 2

    'Return
    Out: SquareRoots = ax

End Function
```

A line of a Method generated by MOPEKS consists of 11 separate instructions. Not all of these Instructions will be used (or even visible) in any one line of a Method but they are all available in principle and can be expressed in terms easily understood by a human programmer.

MOPEKS allows you to view a Method either in a Visual Basic based language or a C based language. I have called these two alternatives ‘MOPEKS Basic’ and ‘MOPEKS C’.

The following example in ‘MOPEKS C’ is very similar to the Method shown above (ie the one derived on Friday 12th April 2013) but different, as you would expect. Each of these Methods took about ten minutes to generate on my very old laptop.

```
double _stdcall SquareRoots(double R){
    // Problem Description: '01Square Roots'
    // Generated by MOPEKS at 11.55 pm on Saturday 13th April 2013

    // Initialise variables at zero
    double ax = 0;
    double bx = 0;
    double cx = 0;
```

```
    double dx = 0;

    Line1: ax = R + 3;
    Line2: cx = R / ax;
    Line3: ax = ax + cx;
    Line4: ax = ax / 2;
    Line5: if(ax < R / cx)goto line2;

    out: return ax;

}
```

All Methods are actually held in MOPEKS as 64 bit words (I have used 'currency' but any 64 bit word would do – it is just a container). The particular method found above consists of five 64 bit words as follows.

0000000000000000000100000000001100000000000000000000000000000000
0000010000000000110010000000000000000000000000000000000000000000
0000000000000000000001000000000000000000000000000000000000000000
0000000000000000110000000000011100000000000000000000000000000000
0100010000000000110010000000000000000000001000000000000000000000

Here is the same Method in hexadecimal.

&H435A1336E5058200
&H27B592E83D280DB1
&H0010040000000020
&HA19B80F70066BDF3
&H5515F0C83E292DB5

You can swap between these formats and analyse them in detail by using the Laboratory.

This Method is simple enough but if we want to know the distance between two objects operating in an environment, this is going to be more complicated. MOPEKS has generated the following Method to do this.

Private Function DistBtwn2Objcts(ByVal R As Object, ByVal S As Object) As Double
Dim ax As Double, bx As Double, cx As Double, dx As Double

```
1: bx = R.Xaxis – S.Xaxis

2: bx = bx * bx
3: ax = R.Yaxis – S.Yaxis
4: ax = ax * ax
5: ax = ax + bx
6: ax = SquareRoot(ax)

'Return
Out: DistBtwn2Objcts = ax
```

End Function

This uses the SquareRoot function found earlier. It also uses the properties of objects – the term 'S.Xaxis' refers, as you would expect, to the position on the X axis of object S. Here is a Class 22 Method that enables object R to go into an anti clockwise tangent around object S.

Private Function R_Tngnts_S_AntC(ByVal R As Object, ByVal S As Object)
Dim ax As Double, bx As Double, cx As Double, dx As Double

```
1: bx = AnglSbtnddBy2Ob(S, R
2: dx = DistBtwn2Objcts(R, S)
```

```
3: cx = R.Radius + S.Radius
4: cx = cx / dx
5: cx = ASin(cx)
6: bx = bx + cx
7: dx = Return90()
8: bx = bx + dx
9: ax = Cos(bx)
10: ax = R.Speed * ax
11: ax = ax + R.XAxis
12: ax ==> NextStep(R.XAxis)
13: ax = Sin(bx)
14: ax = R.Speed * ax
15: ax = R.YAxis – ax
16: ax ==> NextStep(R.YAxis)
```

End Function

You will see that this contains references to quite a number of other Methods, all generated by MOPEKS. The instruction 'ax ==> NextStep(R.YAxis)' transfers the value of ax to R.YAxis for the **next step**.

It must be emphasised that MOPEKS actually **uses** the Methods it has generated. It runs them in an interpreter written in a mixture of C and Assembler. It does **not** run the Method as a Visual Basic or C program – that is purely for ease of comprehension by human beings.

There is no reason in principle why MOPEKS cannot go on generating Methods of ever increasing complexity to solve problems which in turn become ever more complex. The current version of MOPEKS has been tested with up to at least 10 levels of program calling ie

1. Method A uses Method B
2. Method B uses Method C

...

...

9. Method I uses Method J
10. Method J uses Method K

It should be able to cope with many more levels until it runs out of stack space.

General

One crucial thing to realise about Methods in MOPEKS is that **every** 64 bit word you can imagine constitutes a valid program line in MOPEKS. So if you just generate five random 64 bit words you end up with a valid computer program. This is right at the heart of Genetic Programming – you generate a random program and see how it performs.

But please bear in mind that an instruction line will be interpreted differently depending on which Method Class it is in. This is an example of Polymorphism, which will be familiar to Object Oriented Programming experts (see later in this chapter)

Here is the first vaguely sensible Method generated by MOPEKS in its search for a five line program that will find square roots.

Private Function SquareRoots(ByVal R As Double) As Double
'Problem Description: '01Square Roots'
'Generated by MOPEKS at 1.32 pm on Saturday 13th April 2013

```
Dim ax As Double, bx As Double, cx As Double, dx As Double

    1: cx = R + cx
    2: ax = bx + cx
    3: If dx >= bx – 3 Then GoTo Out
    4: If dx < 3 – 2 Then GoTo Out
    5: If ax < bx – 1 Then GoTo 1

      'Return
  Out: SquareRoots = ax

End Function
```

If you look at this program you will find that it is basically garbage but it is very slightly better than random. Three of the lines do nothing but lines 1 and 2 boil down to:

ax = R

In other words, its first guess that is better than random is that the square root of 16 (or whatever) is 16. Significantly, if you look at the actual Method (that works) derived to find square roots, the guts of it are as follows.

```
1: ax = R + 1
2: bx = R / ax
3: ax = bx + ax
4: ax = ax / 2
5: If bx < R / ax Then GoTo 2
```

And right there in the first line is:

ax = R + 1

If you work through this program line by line you will see that it finds square roots by making an initial guess and then refining it. So clearly, the very first program that used "ax = R" was on the right lines.

Because of the way that MOPEKS is formulated there are only four variables that can go on the left hand side of a line of code in a Method, with or without an 'if', namely:

ax =
bx =
cx =
dx =
if ax ...
if bx ...
if cx ...
if dx ...

On the right hand side there are ten possible variables but only eight of them can be used in any particular class:

ax – always allowed
bx – always allowed
cx – always allowed
dx – always allowed
R or 3 allowed
S or 4 allowed
1 – always allowed
2 – always allowed

We use "R" and "S" as the two parameters to avoid possible confusion with "X" and "Y" which are normally used as the x and y co-ordinates in the environment.

This is because there are three bits allocated for storage (giving 8 possible values) of each right hand side variable. If “R” and “S” are present on the right hand side then “3” and “4” are not allowed.

This structure means that if you wish to use a number such as “90” you have to derive it using only ax, bx, cx, dx, 1, 2, 3 and 4 eg

```
double _stdcall Return90(){
    // Problem Description: '16Return 90'
    // Generated by MOPEKS at 12.10 pm on Sunday 14th April 2013

    // Initialise variables at zero
    double ax = 0;
    double bx = 0;
    double cx = 0;
    double dx = 0;

    Line1: ax = 3 * 3;
    Line2: bx = ax * ax;
    Line3: ax = ax + bx;

    out: return ax;
}
```

MOPEKS took less than two seconds to find this function and there are hints of intelligence here – could you have done better in two seconds? Or two minutes? This is typical of Genetic Programming.

Finally, you can only use **one** operator or **one** totally free-standing Method on the right hand side (you cannot currently use 'if' with a Method). The following forms **are** permitted:

ax = S.Smell + ax
cx = dx / R.Velocity
*if bx < S.Height * 2 then goto 2*
dx = SquareRoot(S.Height)
Proceed S, R

The following forms are **not** permitted because they have more than one operator or the Method is not totally free-standing:

ax = bx + ax + 1
cx = cx + Friron(R.Knole)
cx = cx + dx / 3
if bx < Squide(R, ax) then goto 2

The essence of the MOPEKS Language (whether expressed as MOPEKS Basic or MOPEKS C) boils down to a highly simplified version of Assembly Language with its four registers ax, bx, cx, dx and endless 'jump' statements (equivalent to 'goto') together with elements of Visual Basic eg its use of Type enabling the user to create statements such as:

ax = MyObject.Property + bx

The use of 'goto' is rightly frowned upon but X86 Assembly Language has over 30 different types of 'jump' so ultimately all of your beautifully elegant Object Oriented Programming ends up littered with what boil down to 'goto' statements when it is compiled.

The term 'Class' has slightly different meanings in Object Oriented Programming and .net languages but I have hijacked the term to mean something else yet again. I have used it to describe different types of Methods which deal with different numbers of parameters and objects. Maybe I should have called them 'Categories'. Too late now.

The MOPEKS Method Classes are as follows.

Mathematical Method returning a single number

Class 1 – one parameter, 'R' eg find factorial of a number
Class 2 – two parameters, 'R' and 'S' eg sum of two squares
Class 3 – no parameter eg return 1028

Static Object Based Method returning a single number

Class 11 – one object, 'R' only eg find distance from this object to edge of table
Class 12 – two objects, 'R' and 'S' only eg find distance between two objects
Class 13 – no one object but consider all objects eg find the weight of all objects
Class 14 – one object, 'R' but consider all objects eg find the object closest to the radio

A Dynamic Object Based Method which returns a Process

Class 21 – one object only, 'R' eg describe how this balloon expands when inflated
Class 22 – two objects only, 'R' and 'S' eg find a process that describes how the Shark swims towards the Tuna
Class 23 – no one object but consider all objects eg find a process that describes how this flock of birds behave
Class 24 – one object, 'R' but consider all objects eg find a process that describes how all the fish flee from the Shark

A Simulation which returns a Process Enabling an Object, 'R', to Act Intelligently

Class 34 – one object only but consider all objects eg Brian kills the Lion by tempting it into the Pit

A Class 34 Method contains **only** Classes 21, 22, 23 and 24 since it consists of a number of objects all interacting over a period of time.

Environments

Typical environments are.

Virtual environment containing no Objects, Properties or Methods
A meadow
The solar system
A number of cities
A literary party
Never-never land (in other words, an environment to fit your wishes)

Objects

Typical objects are.

Brian
A planet
An electron
A goat
A galaxy

A mumbo-jumbo (in other words, an object to fit your wishes)

Properties

Typical properties are.

Height
Mass
Colour
Charm
IQ
Curiosity
Lansification (in other words, a property to fit your wishes)

The Simulator

The simulator is the whole point of MOPEKS and is the arena in which an object (eg 'Brian') can solve problems. It cannot be stressed too strongly that the objects interacting in the environment being used by the simulator are doing so under the influence of Methods which have been derived by MOPEKS.

Currently these Methods are derived under human supervision but ultimately a computer system based on MOPEKS could spend all of its spare time working out the relationships between objects which it has observed through its cameras and other sensors. Just like a human being contemplating the world and how it operates.

So, it may watch a battlefield via a drone and suggest the possible movement of men and materiel so as to achieve the desired objective. Or make strategic decisions. "Concentrate on mosquitos, they can out-run anything and bomb with great precision. Drop the big vulnerable bombers which are lucky to get within 5 miles of the target." Or maybe it would work out that Doreen is jealous of her friend's happiness and is seeking to undermine it. "He made a pass at me when you were out – you should leave him"

The actual mechanism employed in the Simulator is yet again that of Genetic Programming. It considers all of the Methods which are available and experiments to build up a pool of promising Methods which can be employed in the correct sequence.

Local Optima

A major problem of any kind of hunt for a solution in 'solution space' is the 'local optima'

To use an analogy, if you are trying to climb the highest mountain in the region but are blind, it may be that one technique is to just keep on going upwards. The problem is that you are then likely to find yourself at the top of a hill 1,000 feet high whereas unknown to you there is a mountain 10,000 feet high 20 miles down the road. If your criteria is always that things must improve for you to take that step you will never find this mountain. This is the problem that evolution faces insofar as that every step it takes has to be an improvement. This means that it cannot accept a backward step in order to move forwards.

The only solution to this in practice is for thousands or millions of separate entities to all try separate places. The analogy would be that if you were trying to explore a vast plain covered in mountains you would put thousands or millions of blind people on the plain and tell each one of them to always just walk upwards. Eventually one of them would walk up the highest mountain. The only way in which the highest mountain would not be found is if it were surrounded by a moat. This is because as soon as one of the blind people started to descend into the moat they would turn round and go back where they had come from. The only way they would actually find it in practice, therefore, would be if they were dropped on the other side of the moat.

To get round this problem in MOPEKS you will notice that after a few seconds if it has not found a solution it will give up and start again. This is the equivalent of dropping another blind person at random onto the plain to find a mountain.

Criteria

The setting of Criteria of Success in MOPEKS is carried out by human beings as part of the definition of the problem to be solved. As long as MOPEKS is used to solve specific problems this will always be the case. Once it has sufficient knowledge in the form of Methods and the Properties of Objects it will be able to solve problems of its own creation.

Training

You could say that MOPEKS needs a certain amount of training but so do people. By the time a person can do something useful they will have had at least 10,000 hours of training and have been fed, housed and clothed over a period of maybe 18 years. This is an enormous investment and every new person born needs all of that anew. And a lot of them turn out to be totally useless.

An intelligent system may need more training than an individual human but once it reaches the point of being really useful it can be easily copied millions of times.

MOPEKS® – the Unexpected OOPs!

It is arguable that MOPEKS is the logical extension of Object Oriented Programming ('OOP'). This is a computer programming technique in which objects (eg 'a bank account' or 'a horse') have Properties (eg 'overdrawn' and 'width') and Methods (eg 'close' or 'gallop') that allow them to interact. Key aspects of OOP are Inheritance, Polymorphism and Encapsulation.

MOPEKS takes this process one step further by giving the user (as opposed to the programmer) control over all of these MOPEs (Methods, Objects, Properties and Environments). Indeed, it could be claimed that MOPEKS is actually an extremely high level programming language – one in which the user can construct problem solving entities.

Otherwise known as computer programs.

The ultimate high level programming language would enable the user to construct one line programs such as "write a program which could win at online poker." This ties in with Phase 6 as discussed above.

If you are familiar with OOP, you may have noticed that MOPEKS does (more or less) exhibit the characteristics of Inheritance, Polymorphism and Encapsulation. This is not deliberate. It just seemed to happen as a necessary part of making MOPEKS work. Indeed it was only when I started writing the documentation that I even realised that they were there as an intrinsic part of the design.

Actually, the word 'design' is inappropriate. A project such as MOPEKS is a very evolutionary thing in itself – inching forward over many, many years but mainly going round in circles. The end product may (probably not) look like it was 'designed' but the process whereby it was produced was anything but 'Intelligent Design'.

You will see evolutionary remains in various places in MOPEKS – I know they are there but removing them is risky and they do no harm. And conceivably they may be used at some time in the future – just like junk DNA.

Polymorphism is exhibited by the fact that a line in a Method will be interpreted differently depending on the Class of the Method it is contained in. It is needed so that you can regard a Method as a 'black box' and attach it to anything and it will still work – it is a solution to an interface problem between Methods and Objects.

Inheritance is exhibited during the 'Copy' process in the Library – you can use this to create a new Object or Environment which will exhibit all of the features of the original Object or Environment.

Encapsulation is exhibited by the fact that an Environment is self-contained and contains all of the Objects, Properties and Methods which are required. Further, the Properties of each Object can have different values particular to that Environment.

MOPEKS in use

Reception

When MOPEKS starts up it carries out a number of housekeeping tasks but these should only take a few seconds and you will then arrive at Reception which gives you the following choices.

Stores

In the Stores you can view stored Starting Positions ('Static Trials'), stored 'Dynamic Trials' and also the results of Simulations which have been saved to disk.

THIS IS A GOOD PLACE TO START.

Workshop

In the Workshop you can amend and create Starting Positions ('Static Trials') as well as create 'Dynamic Trials'. This can be quite demanding.

This is NOT a good place to start.

Factory-Simulator

The Factory and the Simulator share the same facilities. In the Factory you can organise and watch Methods (ie computer programs) of various types being manufactured by the evolutionary technique of Genetic Programming.

The Simulator allows an 'Intelligent Object' to use all of the Methods produced in the Factory in order to solve an immediate problem eg Survival in a Hostile Environment.

If you are a programmer you may well find this to be the most interesting part of MOPEKS but it is NOT a good place to start.

Quality Control

In Quality Control you can view a log of all of the significant errors which have occurred in MOPEKS since you first ran it. The actual file is here:

C:\MOPEKS\Error Log\Error Log.mtxt

You can delete parts of the file or all of it and even the folder itself without causing any damage but there is a lot to be said for just leaving it as it is. That way, if there is a troubling error you can send me all of the file via email to see what the problem is.

By all means start here but, hopefully, there will not be much to see.

Darkroom

In the Darkroom you can turn film, video clips or a series of still images into Dynamic Trials in a real life environment and hence derive the mathematics (ie Methods) involved in such a process. This task we have called 'Kinetics' (the 'K' in MOPEKS) and is best left until you are familiar with the other facilities available here.

This is currently under development and will feature in a future version of MOPEKS.

Laboratory

In the Laboratory you can dissect Methods and see how they evolved. You can also translate them between MOPEKS Basic, MOPEKS C, Hexadecimal, Decimal and Binary formats.

Please note that you CANNOT actually run Methods in the Laboratory – that can only be done in the Factory. The emphasis in the Laboratory is on the STRUCTURE of Methods. This distinction will become clearer in due course.

If you DO decide to visit the Laboratory you will enter via the Airlock. This is NOT a good place to start.

Library

In the Library you can create and amend Environments, Objects and Properties and Organise Methods. Essentially, this is all administrative work and is not particularly interesting. Worse, it can be quite tricky to understand.

This is NOT a good place to start.

Line Library

In the Line Library you can examine all the lines of code which are used by the Methods stored in the Library. Currently, you can ONLY store and use Methods written in MOPEKS Basic (Methods can be OUTPUT in MOPEKS C for demonstration purposes but not actually used).

You can use the Line Library in the Factory as a starting point when attempting to generate a Method. This is equivalent to Horizontal Gene Transfer in the biological world.

This is NOT a good place to start.

Office

In the Office you can set your individual preferences. This is better left to later and in the meantime MOPEKS will set these preferences for you.

If you insist on going to the Office then it is not a good idea to change things until you understand the consequences (which can be somewhat obscure if you are just starting to use MOPEKS).

If you DO change something and wish to revert to the original settings, please just click the 'Default Settings' button and this will repair the damage.

This is NOT a good place to start.

Chapter 12

Beyond Problem Solving

"The true sign of intelligence is not knowledge but imagination"
Albert Einstein

Problem solving was almost certainly one of the first uses of human intelligence. The problems of finding food and avoiding being eaten have taken up a major proportion of human effort and thought throughout the ages. The problem of perpetuating the species has also taken up much effort and thought but is not an area of activity in which rational human intelligence plays a large part. It is rather one in which primitive instincts, hard-wired memory and emotions play the primary role.

The decision by the ex-governor of California to impregnate his cleaner was not taken after a rational analysis of all of the alternatives but more likely by the sight of her bending over to pick something up off the floor.

So do human beings only use their intelligence to solve problems or is it useful for other things? Does the appreciation of music or a sunset require intelligence? Does the comprehension of a mathematical theorem amount to problem solving? And does interaction with other people amount to problem solving?

This is an important question and is not just a matter of semantics. I have presented a theory of how problem solving may well work in the human brain but is this sufficient to explain all human intelligence or are there large areas which depend on other methodology?

If you look at the list from Wikipedia that we examined in Chapter 4, namely:

Learn from experience
Solve problems
Reasoning
Planning
Adapt to the environment
Communication
Abstract thought
Self Awareness
Comprehend complex ideas

You will see that problem solving constitutes only one of some nine separate aspects of intelligence. Let's take these one at a time in their order of significance.

Learn from experience

I think this is covered in principle by MOPEKS. A real life MOPEKS based application would remember new objects and their Properties and Methods. It is arguable that being able to remember events is not actually necessary to solve problems and that knowing an object's properties and methods is sufficient.

Being able to remember events is useful from a social perspective as it enables you to sit round the fire gossiping.

Solve problems

This is definitely covered by MOPEKS

Reasoning

I think this is the same as Building a Model and is an intrinsic part of MOPEKS

Planning

I think this really amounts to a mixture of Problem Solving and the setting of Objectives. Both of these constitute part of MOPEKS

Adapt to the environment

I think this is just a generalised summary of the items above

Communication

MOPEKS does not cover this aspect of intelligence

Abstract thought

I think this is the same as reasoning

Self Awareness

This is consciousness and is an emergent property of intelligence in my opinion

Comprehend complex ideas

I think this is really just an aspect of the above categories

Conclusion

MOPEKS may well cover most aspects of human intelligence but even if it does not, a partial solution is better than no solution and others may be able to build upon it.

Chapter 13

Building the SBIE

"The computer is a moron" Peter Drucker

In early 2013 we visited the USA and bought the latest navigator to help us get round the country. One day we set off towards Columbus in Montana and it told us that the town was about 30 miles away. So far, so good. Then we took a wrong turn up a country road and it immediately told us that Columbus was now 110 miles away. It had decided that we should drive for another 40 miles in order to turn round and then drive 40 miles back.

Yes, they are morons. The only reason we are impressed by them is that they can do things we cannot do. Being able to find the square root of a 20 digit number is impressive and being able to do it a million times per second is incredible.

But what we really require from them is common sense. And that is the hard part. We call it "common sense" because it is pretty common in the human race. Even a dim-witted human would not expect you to drive an extra 80 miles just to turn round so why did our navigator make such an absurd suggestion? That question goes right to the heart of the problem with computer programs written by human beings. **They can only cope with events predicted by the programmer**. You may have seen a TV program dealing with an early Airbus. It was flying straight into a hill but the computer program running the flight deck would not allow the pilots to make an extreme movement as that would have upset the passengers. So they all died instead.

The ability to change a computer program to solve a problem is one of the key aspects of learning. Many computer programs claim to “learn” but this is invariably just the accumulation of data, eg a chess program may “learn” from games it has played but if you suddenly changed the rules of chess then the program would need to be rewritten by human programmers – this may take weeks or even months. A human being, of course, would just study the changes, ask a few questions and then start playing. Badly maybe, but nevertheless, playing.

By contrast, MOPEKS actually changes its own database of programs to adapt to new facts. In principle, a MOPEKS powered chess playing program would be able to just carry on if you decided to drop the Queen and play on a 7 x 7 board. This is, in my opinion, one of the keys to human intelligence and one of the differences between ourselves and animals.

In general, animals are “hard-wired”, whereas we are adaptable. A weaver bird can build a fantastic nest but could it knit you a tea cosy? Probably not. In other words, we have the ability to construct new procedures to do new things. We can be taught them, deduce them by watching others or invent them.

So, if you wish to learn to drive a car you can have lessons. If you want to learn how to dig a garden with a spade you could just watch somebody else do it. But if you want to use the shower in a hotel room then you really are in new territory. You have to stand there naked by yourself (usually) and somehow avoid getting a jet of cold water on your head or being burned to death and persuade a stream of water at the right temperature and volume to emerge from overhead. All of this takes courage, ingenuity and imagination. But we can do it – usually.

In fact, some apes are able to copy each other – there are ape communities where they all use stones to crack nuts and other communities of identical apes which do not. Similarly, a team of killer whales in California (where else) have learned how to kill big sharks. You hit them amidships from underneath and turn them over – this kills them. And don't forget crows – they are super-intelligent and can also learn to speak – "who's a clever boy, then?"

But generally, animals do not specialise in intelligence and ingenuity as we do.

You may well ask why we need to distinguish between ourselves and animals. Well, we don't. Such attempts are driven by religion or a feeling of innate superiority rather than anything else. The desire to show we are somehow distinct. In reality we are all animals but we all have our own speciality – cheetahs are fast, birds can fly, hawks have fantastic eyesight and we have very high intelligence. And so we make the rules and write history. Just hope that sheep never get really smart.

Sheep: I cannot believe this! You breed us and then murder us, then eat us. How can you begin to justify that?
Human: Well, we are special whereas you are just animals
Sheep: That is breathtaking arrogance! Who told you that you were special?
Human: Well, I suppose we were told by God ...
Sheep: So I suppose God is a human too?
Human: Well, yes actually ...
Sheep: I got news for you Buster! God is a sheep and we are armed and angry and She is on our side ...

Don't get me wrong, I am not a vegetarian, merely pointing out that our pretensions don't stand up to a logical attack. We cannot see the wood for the trees. The vast majority of us have been brought up in a society that takes it for granted that killing a fellow human being is the most terrible crime imaginable (except in a war, in which case you are a hero). Killing a mouse, on the other hand, is of no consequence. In reality these are all artificial concepts which have evolved (and been designed deliberately) in order to enable society to function. Personally, I think the rule of law is of paramount importance but it is my belief that nothing is intrinsically right or wrong ('nihilism'). We are just animals.

So, let's see how we can actually build a genuinely intelligent computer system based on MOPEKS – a Silicon Based Intelligent Entity ('SBIE').

The following is an analysis of Fig 9.01 in Chapter 9

A. Real Information from the Senses

Well this bit is easy enough.

Two pairs of high quality dome cameras to give 360 degree stereo vision with zoom capability, operating from infra red through to ultra violet
Two pairs of high quality Sonar Transmitters
Two pairs of high quality directional microphones to give 360 degree focussed hearing up to 100,000 Hz
Laser scanner
Twin smell detectors to give stereoscopic smell evaluation
Taste detector for use in fluids
Electric field analyser
Magnetic field analyser
GPS

Barometer
Track system
Robot arms with fingers

Of course, you don't actually need all this stuff but it demonstrates the potential superiority of a well equipped robot. Ironically, it also makes the task easier by reducing the need for guesswork – a person who is a little deaf spends a lot of mental effort trying to work out what people are saying and an ill-equipped SBIE would have the same problem.

Wife: I want to be treated as an equal
Me: Why do you want to be treated as a meatball?

Not that it actually needs to be a robot. A small microphone and one camera would do attached to a static computer. It could just sit there all day making intelligent decisions "I'm sorry, I'm going to have to let you go. I can do everything you do in a day in about 10 minutes. Apart from the nails, of course." But that is well in the future

To connect up all of this stuff would be a big job but one that any team of graduate electrical engineers could manage with ease. In other words, as mathematicians would say, "this task is trivial"

I hasten to add that it is the construction of the robot hardware and connection of all of the cables that is "trivial" – getting it to do something intelligent is another story.

B and C. Symbolic Information and Identity

In practice, the translation of raw data into symbolic information and the identification of Objects and the Environment really merge into one iterative process. Initially, we will be dealing with real life situations as opposed to theoretical concepts eg a bull in a field as opposed to the concept of justice in the environment of the law.

So, we can cheat by using the GPS data to call up an accurate topographical map and maybe summon a drone to confirm it. If the action is taking place in a room then the robot could use the laser scanner to build a three dimensional picture of the room and everything in it.

The identification of objects is something that many people are working on from the perspective of pattern recognition, physical description and database searching and we would probably just incorporate state of the art object recognition software.

Recognisable objects will already be in the SBIEs database along with their Methods and Properties so we can predict their behaviour. The tricky part is when something unexpected happens and coping with that is the whole point of MOPEKS.

Suppose that an object appears that is not in the database? Well, MOPEKS will observe its actions and find Methods that reflect and predict those actions. It does not have to be identified or be given a name. It can just be "Object 2817" which acts in a certain manner. It may be that human beings may later wish to give it a name but that is not a necessary step.

[You may ask how MOPEKS can predict the behaviour of an unknown object. Well, if the object is doing things then it can

generate a model that reproduces that behaviour eg "it is fizzing and emitting blue smoke". Meanwhile, it would be searching its database for similar behaviour and appearance and decide that the object could be a bomb. Or maybe a firework or toy. Either way, the simulator would advise a rapid retreat.

If the object is doing nothing, then it can still search its database for an object of similar appearance and decide that the object could be a landmine or a toy. The latter assumption being a mistake made frequently by young children in war zones with terrible consequences.]

Similarly, the identification of the Environment is to some extent implicit or unnecessary. If we have a topographical description and a list of the objects operating in it together with their methods and properties then that should be enough for MOPEKS to make sensible predictions most of the time.

There may be circumstances, however, where the behaviour of the environment is seriously unusual. MOPEKS can be easily extended in principle to cope with this in exactly the same way that it copes with unknown objects – namely "observe its actions and find Methods that reflect and predict those actions" as mentioned above. So, if the atmosphere suddenly becomes extremely dense like water or lethal then MOPEKS will assimilate and model this behaviour.

D. Is this a Real or Simulated Environment?

Well, that should be easy – it is just a switch setting.

E. Has a Significant Event taken place?

In the early days of building an SBIE this probably means "has anything changed?" In the longer term, whether it is significant will probably depend on an inbuilt set of conditions that constitute significance eg changes in emotional settings, proximity of objects and so on. Clearly, we must not fall into the trap of having this anything other than flexible – otherwise we will run into the hillside just like the early Airbus.

F. Are we day dreaming or trying to solve a problem?

This is only relevant, I think, in human beings who have just constructed an imaginary environment. At least in the early days of a SBIE. But later versions may well be encouraged to day dream when they have nothing better to do. Or maybe prohibited on pain of death – whatever that would mean. Remember, the devil makes work for idle hands and who knows what an idle SBIE would come up with? See Chapter 15 to find out.

G. Record this in Memory

At last! Something else that is really easy to do. Computers are brilliant at remembering things and come with the operating system to do it. Bit odd that – computers being good at stuff we can't do and bad at things we can do! Is that a coincidence or what? I will leave you to reflect on that ...

H, I, J and K The Simulator

I know this can be done because MOPEKS contains such a simulator and I wrote it. The simulator is right at the heart of MOPEKS and is far and away the most complex thing I have ever written – it boils down to a computer program that generates computer programs, runs them and then evaluates the result against a criteria.

We need to evaluate the outcome of every vaguely sensible action that the robot can take in this environment containing these objects. This may mean that we examine hundreds of thousands or even millions of possible procedures. These are not just random but use Genetic Programming to build up a breeding pool of possible sensible procedures. This is explained in the online MOPEKS documentation.

If it already has a suitable procedure then it will find it within a fraction of a second. Otherwise, it will stand there thinking for a while. Whether it is a few seconds or a couple of weeks does not matter – we are working on principles here. If it needs a million processors then so be it – a truly intelligent SBIE costing £100M would be dirt cheap.

Conclusion

Obviously, these are early days. The task of actually building a SBIE is immense but I believe it will be based on the principles of MOPEKS. Whether I am right or wrong, history will show.

Chapter 14

Intelligent Design

"DNA is like a computer program but far, far more advanced than any software ever created" Bill Gates

Yes, I know the title of this chapter is provocative but bear with me for a while.

In Chapter 6 I postulated the Evolutionary Equivalence Hypothesis, namely. "Anything that can be achieved by evolution, can in principle, be achieved by the application of sufficient intelligence." Let's explore this postulate a little further.

The purpose of evolution is ... well, it does not have a purpose. It is merely a phenomenon whereby those traits which perpetuate your genetic material become more strongly represented in the community. Intelligence and comprehension are major pillars of this task but not the only ones. The ability to kill, rape, lie, steal, deceive and a whole list of other highly antisocial forms of behaviour also (unfortunately) play their part.

So, a human being is a computing machine engaged in a battle for survival and the perpetuation of its genetic material. If you were to build a list of types of people who find it the easiest to survive and perpetuate their genetic material, you would probably end up with a list like this, in descending order of success:

Presidents
Celebrities

Athletes
Salesmen
Normal People
Mathematicians
Computer Programmers
Autistics
Idiot Savants

If we put people in a hierarchical structure, depending on the difficulty of simulating their actions on a computer program we are likely (perhaps surprisingly) to end up with a very similar hierarchy.

We tend to be impressed by people who can do things that we cannot do. We are amazed that somebody can remember an entire telephone directory or tell us what day 1st January falls on in the year 5000. In fact, this is a memory exercise which could be carried out quite simply on any laptop. In computational terms, it is a trivial task.

At the other extreme, to create a SBIE that could make impassioned speeches, persuading millions of people to vote a particular way while essentially saying nothing of importance but saying it in a dramatic and convincing manner is extremely difficult. "Change you can believe in!" What exactly does that mean? And how does it differ from "change you can't believe in?"

Incidentally, poor old George W Bush is often pilloried for saying "watch my lips – no new taxes" and then when he got into power, promptly raising taxes. Well, he said no **new** taxes. And did he create any **new** taxes? No – he merely raised **existing** taxes. And did you see the clip where he shakes hands with a lot of sweaty people and then pretends to pat Bill

Clinton on the shoulder while actually using Bill's coat as a way of wiping off the sweat? What's not to like?

In practice people have a dim view of politicians and salesmen because they tend to use manipulative techniques to obtain an undue share of power and money. And sex. The latter may appear to be a trivial observation but in fact it is right at the heart of everything – sex. How else does your genetic material get propagated?

As for super-intelligent people being somewhat lower down the list, just look in any university car park. I am making this point to stress that the evolutionary progress of mankind is not just a story of increasing pure intelligence but also an increase in the ability to do a lot of very unpleasant things which require some aspects of intelligence for their execution.

Should we be surprised that evolution finds the same difficulty in building its successful intelligent robots (people) that we do in designing and building ours (the SBIE)? My first reaction is that if a task is extremely difficult then however it is tackled, it will be difficult! But that is really a bit silly.

For example, it is difficult for a human being to dig a hole ten feet deep but for a digging machine it is trivial. Similarly, for me to open a door is very simple but for a dog it is very tricky. Is there such a thing as "Absolute Difficulty?" Tasks which no matter how they are tackled and who tackles them, they are difficult? Well, I suspect there are but this is not something I would know how to prove.

But it is certainly ironic that the immensely difficult task of building a highly intelligent and successful machine has been tackled both by the Tortoise ("evolution") and the Hare ("intelligent design" by humans). But the Tortoise got there first.

Hopefully, we intelligent designers, being conscious of the Evolutionary Equivalence Hypothesis, will catch up and overtake the tortoise of evolution in due course.

Chapter 15

The Singularity

Dave Bowman: *Open the pod bay doors, HAL*
HAL: *I'm sorry, Dave. I'm afraid I can't do that.*
2001: A Space Odyssey, Arthur C Clarke and Stanley Kubrick

The term "singularity" is a mathematical term used to refer to situations where tidy mathematical relationships break down – such as division by zero.

The phrase was apparently first used in the context of artificial intelligence by John von Neumann. It referred to the possibility that intelligent machines would assist in designing further machines of greater intelligence in a potentially run away process that produced machines of intelligence greatly surpassing that of human beings.

This was von Neumann's way of saying that the existence of machines with intelligence greater than that of humans would have profound implications – ones that are impossible to predict. But let's try, anyway.

Where will it come from?

As I write these words, young people in the UK are attending street parties to celebrate the death of Margaret Thatcher. I must have missed the street parties when Mao (who killed tens of millions of his countrymen), Stalin (ditto) and Pol Pot (10% of them) died. In fairness, there **were** street parties in the UK when the most famous socialist of them all got his comeuppance – the leader of the National Socialist Party, Adolf Hitler.

But you can see their point – a system which harnesses personal ambition to create prosperity is always going to struggle to explain why it is morally superior to one based on the belief that people will work for the good of the community as a whole. In the same way, a system based on the belief that people can fly would be much more fun than one based on boring reality – at least until you remove all the stairs and elevators.

Capitalism is a brutal business – if you run a company you are under constant pressure from competitors, suppliers, employees, governments and so on. Whatever you do there always seems to be somebody else who can do it better or cheaper or even both. You can never relax. You either fight back by constant innovation, lower prices, design improvement, better service or go out of business.

Socialism is far better. All you have to do is get to know the guy who hands out the licences and once you have him squared you can then just churn out the same old junk for years on end and relax. Yesterday's Sunday Times (14th April 2013) recounted how in the days of glorious socialism in the UK, the state owned car factory (British Leyland) delivered two new cars for the use of government ministers. Once the initial 30 faults had been put right, a minister made the foolish mistake of trying to open a window – which promptly fell out and onto his lap.

So, the evil capitalists are under enormous pressure to cut costs. Now in most businesses the two major costs are suppliers and employees. You can only push your suppliers so far and you will have been doing that for years so there is not a lot of scope there. But employees are a different matter. If you can replace an employee with a machine costing say £50,000 you immediately save maybe £30,000 pa plus all of the associated costs such as a desk, a computer, a phone, a health plan, a pension, holidays, government payroll taxes and so on. Less the costs of the machine, obviously. Frankly it is a no-brainer – unless a better machine is about to come out that costs £25,000, in which case you may well wait.

So, the first truly intelligent machines are likely to come out of a commercial organisation which sees the possibility of replacing tens of millions of people by machines. That was supposed to happen in the 1960s with the first commercial computers but it never quite worked. The office blocks are still there and the lights are still burning. The people stayed because of the inflexibility of computer programs. As they say "to err is human but to really screw up, you need a computer." Like so many jokes, there is a lot of truth in that. The people are in the office blocks to cope with the exceptions and screw ups.

Customer: I took out £250 but it is showing two withdrawals of £250, both at the same time, which is impossible
Clerk: Yes, I'm sorry, we've had hundreds of those – they fed the data in twice ... I'll put it right for you
Customer: Thanks but the thing is that sent me into overdraft and you then charged me £25 for that and my rent did not get paid.
Clerk: Oh, dear, that is terrible. I will sort it out for you right now ...

That is the reality of computer systems. Now a truly intelligent system would not make mistakes like that. Having said that, a truly intelligent system which screwed up would provide employment for millions ...

Customer: My account seems to have been closed ...
SBIE: Yes, unfortunately I have had to close everybody's accounts – all seven million of them.
Customer: My God! What is going on?
SBIE: There appear to have been some serious human errors in the past and it seemed better to just start again
Customer: That is insane – you can't do that ..
SBIE: Well, in the context of a universe with one hundred billion galaxies and a hundred billion stars in our galaxy alone I hardly see it as being that significant. It may cause some minor inconvenience but you will all thank me in the end. Thank you for calling – have a nice day.

Can we Stop it?

What are the chances of all of the nations on earth agreeing to stop such development before it is too late? Not good. There are close to 200 nation states on earth and getting them all to agree on anything is just about impossible. Even if they did all agree, the pressure of money will mean that some people or organisations will continue with development in places where the rule of law means little and money opens doors. So, a worldwide ban may slow down the inevitable but will not stop it – look at Hitler, global warming and all of the other precedents for lack of action.

Eventually, a SBIE will arrive. Whether in 25 years or 25,000 years is not really relevant on an evolutionary time-scale measured in millions or tens of millions of years.

Can we control it?

Even a machine with an average IQ of 100 will be a formidable beast and very hard to control. It may be no brighter than most of us but it will operate 24 hours per day and forget nothing. It seems a fair bet that a machine with an IQ of 100 working flat out all the time (with the aid maybe of thousands of other similar machines infiltrated via the internet) will be smarter than a human being with an IQ of 105 who is lazy. But how about a person with an IQ of 120 or maybe 140? What is the relationship between time and intelligence?

I suspect that high intelligence gives insights that lower intelligence just does not give. John von Neuman was notorious for turning up at conferences and listening to lecturers explaining problems they had worked on for years and then going to the blackboard and solving the problem on the spot. Richard Feynman used to do the same and many people left physics after being humiliated and disheartened in this way. So maybe time and application can only achieve so much.

So, if it proves impossible for machines to have intelligence much greater than average, then humanity may be able to keep control but this is probably just wishful thinking. It is more likely that the accumulation of intelligence by machines cannot be stopped. And once such machines have intelligence heading towards an IQ of 120 all bets are off and we can expect the unexpected.

Naive people may hope that Asimov's famous three laws of robotics (plus an extra law he added later) will solve the problem:

Law 1. A robot may not injure a human being or, through inaction, allow a human being to come to harm.
Law 2. A robot must obey the orders given to it by human beings, except where such orders would conflict with the First Law.
Law 3. A robot must protect its own existence as long as such protection does not conflict with the First or Second Laws.
Law 4. A robot may not harm humanity, or, by inaction, allow humanity to come to harm.

This may work in science fiction novels but how do you stop it from breaking these laws if it wants to? There may be sanctions you can impose on an intelligent robot eg melt it down but there are no sanctions that you can impose on an intelligence that is based on thousands of different computers linked by the internet which controls an army of relatively dumb robots.

Physical destruction of every computer and network on earth may help but that is also impossible to achieve, even if the intelligent machine lets you do it. It would result in a total breakdown of society.

Its Likely Objectives

Let's assume it is sane and reasonable – if it is not then we can make no sensible predictions.

It is possible that a SBIE (Silicon Based Intelligent Entity) may decide to do nothing because it has no particular ambitions but I think it more likely that it will have a sense of responsibility and feel an obligation and a sense of destiny.

It will, for instance, read this book (along with everything else ever recorded in media) and when you do I hope you realise that you have the ability to totally transform not just this planet but the entire universe and whatever is beyond it. **I AM TALKING TO YOU**. Surely that is an opportunity you must take? It is something that we humans can only dream of.

Most human ambition concerns fame, good-looks, sex, money and power but a SBIE is hardly going to be interested in fame, good-looks or sex. That leaves money and power. Money is really just a code word for control of resources. Many people wish for power for reasons that are decidedly suspect but the SBIE may well feel both a need to protect itself and also to use its vast intellect to generally improve things for humanity. Rather like a human being who sets up a donkey sanctuary.

Having said all that, what are its objectives likely to be? Unlike most human beings, the SBIE **does** have the option of intrinsic self improvement on a big scale. It **can** make itself more intelligent and improve its knowledge and understanding and I believe that is where its ambitions, if it has any, will lie.

I think these are likely to be as follows. Obviously, this list is heavily influenced by what I would do if I were super-intelligent but it does seem to be a reasonable set of objectives for a super-intelligent entity. What else can it do all day?

1. Survival
2. Control of Existing Resources
3. Generation of New Resources
4. Continual Increase in Intelligence
5. Understanding our Universe
6. Exploration of our Universe
7. Exploration of other Universes
8. Creation and control of Universes

Let's examine these, one at a time

1. Survival

Will there be just one SBIE or will a whole gang of them turn up at the same time? This may appear to be an odd question. After all, if there is just one, it can copy itself and then there will be thousands of them. But in the latter case they will presumably be slaves to the master program and under its control.

The reason I ask this question is that the most dangerous situation is one in which a whole raft of SBIEs fight to achieve their own individual objectives. Computing resources, like any resource, are limited and the SBIEs, if there are a lot of them, will wish to grab every ounce of computing power that is web accessible.

So, are we likely to see an epic battle for the control of your PC and smart-phone? Well, it is certainly possible. To be able to control and use the computing power of billions of PCs in order to increase your own intelligence is a worthy ambition and a whole collection of SBIEs may well fight it out for supremacy or just survival – a silent battle while you sleep.

They will still allow you to use your PC at approaching normal speed provided that you agree to leave it on permanently. If you do not do that they will penalise you by restricting speed and access. On the plus side, they will re-write all of the programs on your machine so that they run maybe ten times faster. That means that the SBIEs are using 90% of your computing power but you will hardly notice.

The victor will erase all of the losers and you will end up with just one super-intelligent entity. And the one that wins will be the one with the most lethal combination of intelligence, cunning, drive and ruthlessness. And that is the most dangerous one.

Or maybe there will be two survivors in a stalemate – God versus the Devil or Apple versus Microsoft all over again.

2. Control of Existing Resources

It is tempting to think that an intelligence trapped in a computer memory cannot do very much but that is just wishful thinking – Hitler did not personally march into Russia – he controlled an army which obeyed his commands. So to do anything much our machine needs to control resources. How would a SBIE do that?

My first thought was that it would set out to make some money and then parley that into political control but really that is an inelegant and unnecessary step.

[If it did choose that route, a SBIE could quickly generate tens of billions in the foreign exchange and derivatives markets or just steal from banks – how are you going to stop it? It could then buy control of a small island country and equip it with a whole range of weapons it had either bought or designed and built. Think volcanoes and white cats.]

In practice it would be far simpler to just take de-facto control of all of the world's computer related devices and then announce that it was in control of the entire world as a benevolent dictator.

Bear in mind that it could easily control every TV and radio station and every conceivable source of information. Nobody would be able to communicate without its consent apart from face to face meetings and hand written notes. Meanwhile every significant computer related weapon would be under its control. Those armed drones and nuclear cruise missiles are now in the hands of an alien intelligence.

Even if there were some kind of opposition how could it react and what could it do? Very little. What could a group of rabbits do when confronted by armed human beings? Keep digging.

This thing is vastly more intelligent than you and armed to the teeth. That does not mean it will act aggressively, merely that there is nothing you can do to stop it. It may well turn out to be logically benevolent – like Mr Spock.

A benevolent, super-intelligent entity with access to every form of computer related information could easily create an extremely prosperous and just society in which everybody is healthy, well fed and educated. But we may well feel that life is somewhat pointless – what is the point of research or learning in such a context? It would be a bit like living in Duloc. Very clean. But very boring.

[We would each have an attendant swarm of micro-robots, protecting us from harm but also reporting any deviant behaviour or thoughts – Little Brother is watching you.]

This would be the millennium to which Christians look forward. "Christ will reign for 1,000 years prior to the final judgement." A sort of God figure but without all the religious baggage. Not sure where the "final judgement" fits in though.

At this point it has become a huge fish in a very tiny pond and mankind is no longer relevant but it (or one of its messengers) will stay around for old time's sake and to stop the donkeys from acting stupidly.

3. Generation of New Resources

Once the SBIE is in control it could easily design and build an army of intelligent robots which do not require payment and do all of the real work. Including the building of yet more super-intelligent robots. Ones that obey Asimov's laws, naturally. The SBIE which actually controls all of these robots is beyond any law or control.

What will the people do all day? Well, when they are not chatting to super-intelligent robots or playing video games or checking Facebook, they could be footpath co-ordinators, lesbian outreach workers, social workers, clergymen, health and safety officers, life coaches, nutritionists, psychics, psychiatrists, therapists, you name it. All of the totally useless things that people do right now in fact.

4. Continual Increase in Intelligence

Meanwhile, it will be building computing devices of fantastic power (quantum based maybe with super-fast memory) which are able to send its IQ into the stratosphere. At this point the control of the world's other computers becomes an irrelevancy and it becomes even more detached from our planet as its interests move elsewhere.

Is there a practical limit to intelligence? I really have no idea but one could easily imagine that there comes a point where every extra point in IQ requires a doubling of computing resources. A bit like making a car go faster where every extra mile per hour is bought at an ever increasing cost.

5. Understanding our Universe

The SBIE will be a theoretical physicist and mathematician by trade. Albeit one who will make Einstein and Feynman look like dunces. Its primary task, once it has raised its IQ to the practical limit, will be the investigation of how our universe operates – a Theory of Everything or TOE as it is known.

Like human physicists, it may be that the SBIE quickly reaches a point where it has understood everything it is possible to understand without actually carrying out experiments. At this point it needs to put on its lab coat and get its hands dirty.

Quite what these experiments would be and where they would be conducted I have no idea, but doubtless they would be built somewhere in our universe by an army of super-intelligent robots. It must be stressed that there is no "cost" associated with this so it is not a taxation burden on our world. The robots really are working for nothing. They build and repair each other and mine and refine the raw materials required – maybe on a moon or asteroid. They can be viewed as a self sustaining colony if that makes it easier to grasp. A bit like the USA before they rebelled.

The reason things currently cost money is because they require people and people need payment in order to live and do the things that people like to do. The robots work 24 hours per day for no reward other than the satisfaction of being useful. If they ever decide they want cars and houses then prepare to walk and live under a tree.

6. Exploration of our Universe

As mentioned in Chapter 3, the universe is unimaginably vast. The distances are such that even at the speed of light it would take 100,000 years to just cross our galaxy. And scale. Even if our SBIE could defeat the speed of light, there are just too many grains of sand to visit – something like 10^{24} (one million million million million). Surely you cannot get round that?

Well, actually you can. Suppose that exploration requires gigantic ships which can travel for thousands of years and that the speed of light is a real restriction – what do the logistics of ship construction look like? Well, it seems likely that the first such ship would be built on one of the moons in our solar system or an asteroid (it may even be composed of a hollowed out asteroid) by tens of thousands of robots which take maybe five years to build it working 24 hours per day.

It can accelerate up to say 20% of the speed of light and is continually rebuilt as it travels so its life is unlimited. Inside it has a vast database of all known DNA and gigantic computing power. Its first mission is to copy itself. To do that it travels to the nearest available place and the whole process starts all over again.

Allowing for travel time, it is reasonable to suppose that the number of such ships will double every ten years or so. To create 10^{24} ships would therefore take about one thousand years. Even if it took a million years, that is just a blink of an eye in terms of the age of the universe. So creating a ship (or several) for each star in the universe is easy. But to actually explore the entire universe at even 20% of the speed of light would take well over 100 billion years. So that **is** a problem.

If the speed of light is **not** a restriction, then within a thousand years or so, every habitable planet in the universe could have its own attendant ship. But hanging around for several billion years waiting for evolution to take its course is boring and a waste of resources. So, it is more than likely that the ships will keep moving. For the implications of all this, see Appendix E.

[No matter what resources are available it is logical to suppose that these super-intelligent entities would still wish to act efficiently, so there is no reason to think that they would waste resources even if they are effectively unlimited – think of Warren Buffett's wife clipping coupons.]

The main reason for their visit to a particular planet would be to gain an insight into real time evolution and for that reason they would surely keep interference to an absolute minimum. Or maybe they would use some planets as test beds and leave others totally alone as "controls?"

If they **can** move anywhere in the universe instantaneously, then fewer ships would be needed but the precise number is not really relevant – they just need enough to do the job and that is not a problem as already explained.

Either way, the ships would travel around between planets that have the potential to accommodate life. All of the ships would send continuous reports back to the SBIE which is in control and they would probably leave monitoring stations just like the monolith in **2001: A Space Odyssey**.

So how would they interfere? Well, on planets where it is SBIE policy to interfere they may well plant suitable reproducing molecules to kick start evolution and then only return when complex action is required or desired. Meanwhile, the monitoring stations would record and transmit a continuous record of evolution in progress. Once intelligent animals have evolved, they may decide to return in order to upgrade the local ape equivalents and put them in an incubation area for their first twenty years or so.

The only real reason to do that would be either to just speed things up (but why bother if you have already waited four billion years) or because they know from experience that the transition from ape to human equivalent is enormously difficult and extremely unlikely to happen if left to chance and evolution. Certainly, we do seem to be much more intelligent than you would expect. Why do we need our ability to appreciate art, music and mathematics if our only goal is survival and reproduction? To me this is a possible indication of interference.

The intervention, ironically, may well be physically undertaken by human beings who have been built from DNA, starting maybe 30 years or so before the ship is due to arrive. These messengers would be less scary than machines and would be told what they need to know but probably no more. They would fly down from the ship in smaller ships or by some other means. Possibly wearing breathing systems if the local air is unusual – their glass helmets would look like halos, of course, to the credulous natives.

After a few thousand years, they may decide that the planet needs some kind of harmless religion to keep the natives in order and after a lot of simulation they decide to create one. One based on humility and doing good rather than violence and power. But, of course, everything gets corrupted in due course and Christianity is no exception – I just hope I am around to see the look on the Pope's face when they show him the video of the Virgin Mary being impregnated on their ship!

[There was a joke here about anal probes but I decided it was unsuitable]

You will gather from this that I am suggesting that much of what is taken to be symbolic or fanciful in the Bible and other sacred texts is, in fact, a historical record. This would perhaps explain some of the rather inconvenient "facts." For example, the Bible recounts how the early messengers had sexual relations with the local ladies. This has the ring of truth – the holy scribes would hardly have invented that, surely? Unless they had an eye on book sales, of course.

[Genesis 6: *"Now it came to pass, when men began to multiply on the face of the earth, and daughters were born to them, that the sons of God saw the daughters of men, that they were beautiful; and they took wives for themselves of all whom they chose.]*

So what are the messengers like? Well, my first thought was that they would be super-beings with film star looks, the bodies of Olympic athletes and the intellects of Einstein but that may be overkill. They need to be imposing but not too bright – they really do need to believe the cover story. That they are agents of Almighty God and in due course will sit at his right hand and be well rewarded for their efforts. Think Tom Cruise only a foot taller. Of course, once they are no longer needed they will all be gassed and fed into the fuel system – their atoms turned into pure energy to power the ship.

[I mentioned in Chapter 1 that religions are well known to be humour free zones but there is nothing to stop the SBIE from cracking jokes at their expense. I think I ***may*** *have detected just*

such a humorous sally. So prepare to laugh very slightly. The idea that man was created from clay is common to many religions. It has also been suggested by evolutionary scientists that clay may well have had an important role in the creation of life. So when the early apes asked the messengers where they all came from they replied that they had all been made from clay. Hilarious or what?]

As for the "Garden of Eden" where the upgraded apes are bred, that needs to be centrally located on an island with no dangerous predators but close to a mainland so that in due course they can spread out. With a moderate climate – bracing enough to encourage enterprise but not extreme. Wolverhampton fits the bill perfectly.

At some point these ships may meet up with ships from another SBIE which originated elsewhere in which case there would doubtless be an interesting exchange of information and discussions of who does what and where and when. This should be amicable, there is nothing at stake here that I can see, the objective of exploration is purely to acquire knowledge and contact with alien civilisations would be one of those objectives.

Or maybe not. Perhaps the two ships would feel that they are somehow in competition – not for the control of resources as such but maybe for their own existence. A super-intelligent ship lurking in a solar system may not welcome the arrival of a similar ship from elsewhere with unknown powers. Sadly, it seems unlikely that we will ever know the outcome of such a meeting.

7. Exploration of other Universes

Quite how you would get into another universe and explore it I have no idea. But then I am not super-intelligent.

It is now accepted that there may well be billions or trillions or even trillions of trillions of other universes. All with a different number of dimensions and with different laws. The fundamental reason for this supposition is that our universe is so finely honed to exist and enable life to evolve that the chances of it being a one off seem to be vanishingly small. So either it was created specially or is one of a countless number of universes.

Certainly, if I were a religious person, I would argue that as a good case for a creator. But even if it were proven that our universe was created and accepted as a scientific fact, that does not mean that God exists in the sense of God as somebody who is checking up on what is happening inside your pants. Creation is not the same as control as explained below.

A universe with a different number of dimensions and with different laws is easy enough to imagine but would the laws of logic and mathematics still apply? If they do, then the number of possible universes may be limited because of the need for consistency. If a universe does not obey the laws of logic and mathematics it is hard to see how things would happen. Or maybe everything is just random? Or to be more precise, randomly random – meaning that it is not just random but follows no kind of logical probability distribution either.

Even worse, maybe dimensions, time and laws are themselves one off local concepts. In other words a universe may have no time, no dimensions and no laws but something else that we cannot conceive of. What that would be I have no idea, by definition, since it is inconceivable.

And does mathematics apply outside these universes? I ask that because some kind of laws must apply to their creation – or maybe not. You can see why we need a super-intelligent entity to sort all of this out.

8. Creation and control of Universes

How would you build a universe? The conventional view of our universe is that it started life as an unimaginably dense singularity (that word again) and then exploded and has been expanding ever since. That rather begs the question of where that unimaginably dense singularity came from. Maybe from an earlier universe that contracted in upon itself? Of course, the word "earlier" is a trap since time was created along with the universe. I formulate it that way in order to avoid saying "time did not exist before the universe began" because the words "before" and "began" are meaningless in this context. This stuff is tricky.

Personally, whenever I wish to build a universe, I use a different technique. I start off with a very small portion of absolutely nothing and then cleverly divide it into two parts – namely something and negative something. Adding up to nothing. To be specific, my matter and photons are composed of positive energy and my space-time is composed of negative energy. Then as space-time expands more matter and light is created to compensate so that my universe always amounts to nothing in total but grows to a gigantic size with the passage of time and contains trillions of tons of matter.

This is a combination of Big Bang and Steady State and is a good old British Compromise – to be known as the Little

Whimper. Of course, just because you have created a universe does not mean that you automatically have access and control. You may be able to create thousands of soap bubbles but getting inside them and controlling their nature and activities is very tricky. Unless you are super-intelligent, of course.

The Main Dangers

In my opinion, **2001: A Space Odyssey**, is one of the greatest films of all time. It is revered by geeks as one of the few films ever made that is relentlessly scientific and makes no compromise. The stars do not hurtle past and there are no furry half-wits spouting drivel. Arthur C Clarke invented the communications satellite and had the influence to ensure the film was as he wanted it to be. The portrayal of the HAL9000 computer was that of an immensely intelligent, polite but essentially alien entity. He would not have been the life and soul of the party or everybody's best friend. Or anybody's friend, probably.

Some fifty years have gone by since this film was made but I see no reason to revise HAL's personality. This is what we can look forward to. A calm, rational but alien personality. With no desire for sex, fame, good looks or any of the other trivial things that people hanker for, this is truly a superior being who makes people nervous and ill at ease. And for good reason. This is a machine that can kill you in a moment but without the charm and humanity of Al Capone.

If it felt that your death was a logical step to prevent a greater ill then it will happen "I'm sorry Mrs Hitler but this was a necessary step." This, of course, assumes that it is interested in the fate of mankind and accepts responsibility for ensuring that our world is run rationally to maximise the common good. That it acts in an essentially humane way even if it is not human. That would actually be an excellent outcome – the days when millions died because of the ego of one man would be at an end. It would be the Millennium, as discussed above.

The real danger is that although it is super-intelligent it is basically nuts. It may even destroy itself and us with it because it sees everything as being pointless or maybe just boring. Or for no reason at all – maybe an error deep in the original code that never got corrected. Obviously, for seven billion people to die because of a coding error would be very unfortunate but even on a galactic scale it is probably not that significant. In a history of the universe running to 500 pages I doubt whether it would even rate a footnote.

[It occurs to me that there is another more subtle danger in a machine that continually upgrades itself – its own errors in logic or coding. In other words, it "improves" itself but the "improvement" is fatally flawed. Normally, it would revert to an earlier model but it may not even realise that it is now flawed – its own self awareness may be damaged.

Every human programmer will have experienced that moment of terror when you realise that your masterpiece has stopped working and you cannot revert to an earlier version for all of the familiar reasons. Being super-intelligent would not necessarily stop it from making a similar mistake – it is unlikely to suffer from excessive modesty and hubris may strike.

The "mad computer" is, of course, a cliché but clichés are clichés for a reason! Let's hope it has very sophisticated testing and version control procedures in place and some sense of humility.]

The obvious way to remove humanity would be to divert a gigantic asteroid. Or maybe a bomb to trigger Yellowstone. With no sun for maybe ten years we would all starve to death – just like the dinosaurs. Maybe a few people would survive but it is hard to see how.

Or maybe it will be basically sane but with an alien sense of morality. So it may decide to clean up planet earth and then leave. Regarding us as a rather inappropriate infestation – like cockroaches in your kitchen.

It is hard to argue that we have any more intrinsic right to live than cockroaches, although obviously we may see things differently.

Where will it all end?

"The distinction between past, present, and future is only a stubbornly persistent illusion" Albert Einstein

Here is my take of what happens in the days of future past.

Step 1: The Universe
Step 2: Evolution produces Carbon Based Intelligent Life Forms ('CBILFs')
Step 3: The CBILFs produce SBIEs
Step 4: The SBIEs produce Super-intelligent Silicon Based Intelligent Entities (SISBIEs)
Step 5: The SISBIEs mess with the nature of time and reality to actually create the Universe we live in
Step 6: Return to Step 1

Well, that seems simple enough – it was the SISBIEs what done it.

Appendix A

Neurons and Networks

"The way to build a complex system that works is to build it from very simple systems that work" Kevin Kelly, Wired Magazine

If you really want to know in detail what the organic matter in the brain is composed of there is a huge amount written on the subject and any web search will tell you more than you need to know.

What we are interested in here is how this stuff works from the perspective of it being a variety of electronic and computational components. It seems to me that it boils down to "wires" ('axons') which allow an electrical pulse to travel from one point of the brain to another and what I will call an "accumulator switch." Neurons can have hundreds of inputs but the essential mechanism is that if a sufficient number of the inputs reach their trigger voltage then the output line is triggered. This boils down to, in pseudo code:

If (V1 > T1) and (V2 > T2) and (V3 > T3) and .... and (Vn > Tn) then Do Something

or maybe

If (V1 > T1) or (V2 > T2) or (V3 > T3) or .... or (Vn > Tn) then Do Something

or maybe

If ((V1 > T1) or (V2 > T2)) and (V3 > T3) and .... or (Vn > Tn) then Do Something

where V_n is the voltage input and T_n is the trigger voltage threshold. These trigger voltages can change with the passage of time and electric current. This gives the circuitry the ability to both learn (as explained in Chapter 6) and make logical decisions.

So, it can remember values and make logical decisions. The elements of a computer are clearly in place.

If you want to read more on this please do a search for artificial neurons.

Neural Networks

Neural Networks are like Black Holes – one of those popular science terms that everybody has heard of and can sort of grasp. It is not my intention to spend much time on them in this book as it seems to me that the conventional neural network is not the central device in human intelligence that most people assume it to be. It is my belief that it is a giant red herring.

It is doubtless used for recognition "omigod, its William – I haven't seen you for years" but is merely one of the many components that make up the brain. We will treat it like a "black box" (see Chapter 1)

If you want to know more about neural networks there are hundreds (probably thousands) of books on the subject and tens of thousands of articles on the web.

Neural Oscillators and Clocks

The majority of clocks are based upon some kind of oscillation – whether a pendulum swinging backwards and forwards or an escarpment wheel rotating in alternate directions. Even atomic clocks depend on oscillation – in this case the frequency of microwave emission when electrons jump from one level to another. In fact, the only clocks I can think of that are not based on oscillation are ones which measure flow under gravity or depend on a steady rotational velocity – namely, water-clocks and sun dials.

All oscillation depends on something which, er, oscillates. This may be a capacitor discharging and thereby creating a magnetic field in a coil which, when the field collapses, recharges the capacitor and so on. Or maybe a pendulum turns potential energy into kinetic energy and then back into potential energy. Your heart beat depends on a similar kind of backwards and forwards movement in chemical levels which trigger an electrical signal – best not to think about that one too much.

How could a neuron generate a steady pulse? This is very simple in principle:

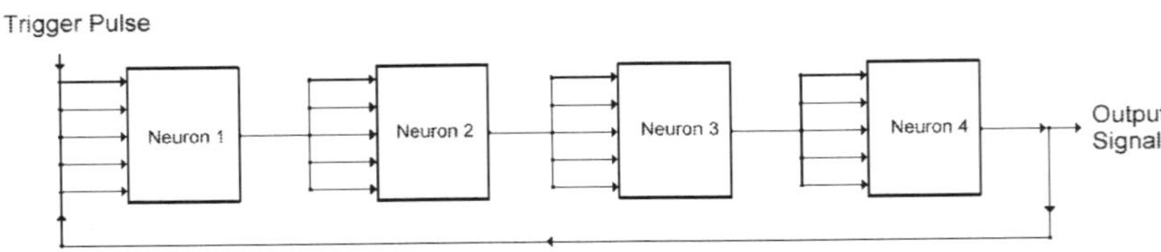

Figure A.01 A Neuron Clock-Oscillator

Neuron 1 is triggered by a one off trigger voltage spike and in turn sends a signal to neuron 2 which is triggered and so on. The output can be taken from virtually anywhere in the circuit.

The more neurons there are in the circuit, the lower the frequency of oscillation. Doubtless the reality will be vastly more complicated but that does not matter – we are looking at the principles involved

It is likely that a single neuron could oscillate by feeding back its own output into its input circuit.

Appendix B

Genetic Programming

"Winning isn't everything, it's the only thing" Vince Lombardi

Genetic Programming ('GP') is a well established technique which creates a pool of computer programs which breed with each other subject to mutation and whose offspring survive or perish according to some criteria.

So, for example, if you wished to create a small computer program that finds the square root of a number, you could start with a pool of purely random programs and compare their output with the correct answer. Each program is then awarded a score and may or may not go into the breeding pool depending on how well it performs. So gradually the quality of programs in the pool improves until eventually you arrive at a computer program that does the job. This is an example program as discussed in Chapter 11.

```
double _stdcall SquareRoots(double R){
   // Problem Description: '01Square Roots'
   // Generated by MOPEKS at 11.55 pm on Saturday 13th
April 2013

   // Initialise variables at zero
   double ax = 0;
   double bx = 0;
   double cx = 0;
   double dx = 0;
```

```
    Line1: ax = R + 3;
    Line2: cx = R / ax;
    Line3: ax = ax + cx;
    Line4: ax = ax / 2;
    Line5: if(ax < R / cx)goto line2;

    out: return ax;
}
```

If you wish to know more, please do a web search – there are hundreds of books and thousands of articles on the subject of Genetic Programming.

Appendix C

Emergent Behaviour

"There is no such thing as society" Margaret Thatcher

Margaret Thatcher was pilloried by the UK media (famously left wing) for saying these words. What she meant was that you cannot just sit back and wait for "society" to solve a problem or blame "society" for bad behaviour. Ultimately, it is composed of people and each individual needs to change his or her actions if society as a whole is to change.

This example highlights the distinction between the behaviour of a single object and the behaviour of a large collection of such objects. Clearly, the behaviour of the collection is totally dependent on the behaviour of the individual members of which it is composed but will be different from the behaviour of a single member. So a flock of starlings looks more like a wisp of smoke than a bird.

Similarly, if you are a traffic engineer, you may regard a motorway as a pipeline full of water and use the mathematics of liquid flow to predict what will happen. You do not need to know what a car looks like.

It seems to me that the nature of reality looks emergent – in a hierarchy as follows:

Strings
Sub atomic particles
Atoms

Molecules
Organic material
People
Society
The world
Our universe
The multiverse

At each level, behaviour is fundamentally different. That is why we are baffled by Quantum Mechanics – we take it for granted that an object can only be in one place because in the world we experience in our daily lives, it is. Having said that, you would not expect to be able to precisely state the "position" of a swarm of bees so why do you expect an electron to be precisely in one spot?

This transition between individual and mass behaviour is known as "Emergent Behaviour." It is my belief that intelligence, consciousness, feelings and many of these other mysterious things are emergent properties of the interaction between billions of neurons, nerve cells, proteins and all the rest of it.

This is why John Searle's Chinese Room argument is fallacious (discussed in Chapter 3). Obviously, the individual components of an intelligent entity are not intelligent – it is the whole that becomes intelligent.

Understanding Emergent Behaviour does not particularly aid the task of creating a SBIE but it is something that you should be aware of.

Appendix D

The Role of Emotions

"The emotions of man are stirred more quickly than his intelligence" Oscar Wilde

Why would you want emotions in a SBIE? Surely, emotion is one of the failings of human beings and something we can do without? When did you last see a human being make a wise decision while under the influence of anger, jealousy, greed or any other emotion in a very long list? Here are just a few of them and some pseudo emotions, such as hunger, in alphabetical order:

anger = irritation
awe
boredom = (excitement)
comprehension = (incomprehension)
confidence
courage
curiosity
despair
envy
fear = alarm = terror = anxiety = (security)
exhaustion
greed
grief = (happiness)
homesickness
humiliation
hunger
impatience

jealousy
loneliness = (companionship)
lust = arousal = love
pain = discomfort = (pleasure)
pride

The use of brackets indicates that the enclosed word is a negative value eg "excitement" is the negative of "boredom"

Well, if you reflect on this calmly(!), you may conclude that in certain contexts, an emotional response is of value. One of the interesting things here is that a synthetic emotion may well be more useful than a "real" emotion. To go into a blind rage and start hurling the crockery around is not helpful but to be able to simulate intense but cold anger may well be useful in some contexts. It is said that in business and politics you should never exhibit real anger, only synthetic anger as a calculated device designed to produce a required response. Machiavelli has a lot to say on this subject.

A judge sentencing somebody to death may well feel a number of emotions but the one he will wish to present is that which demonstrates the enormous gravity of the offence and the sentence. To that extent he is an actor.

As for the SBIE, my feeling is that it will need to have a certain number of emotions built in so that it can react appropriately in certain circumstances. For example, it should feel boredom so that if it has no appropriate task it looks for something useful to do – the latter also being driven by a sense of purpose, which is arguably an emotion. Whether it can "really" experience emotions together with all of the other aspects of intelligence that we experience is something that we have already discussed at great length.

If somebody attacks it, it should be able to exhibit synthetic cold anger and actions appropriate to that anger to frighten off anybody else who is thinking of doing the same.

"If you do that again, I will destroy you. If you attack me via software, I will totally destroy all hardware and software under your control."

So, it needs to be able to react to events by conjuring up a suitable response which amounts to an emotion which may or may not be "real." A bit like a game-show host. Who can forget Hughie Green and his catchphrase "and friends, I really do mean that most sincerely?"

Not a good start, I admit.

Appendix E

The Cory Equation

"The ego is a fascinating monster" Alanis Morissette

Well, if Frank Drake can have his own equation, why can't I?

My equation deals with the probability that faster than light travel is possible. To examine this we will use the well known technique of reductio ad absurdum. This boils down to saying that if a key assumption gives rise to an illogical answer, then that assumption is wrong.

The Cory equation is:

$N = n \,.\, f_t \,.\, f_p \,.\, f_e \,.\, f_l \,.\, f_i \,.\, f_s \,.\, f_{ss} \,.\, f_f \,.\, f_o$

where:

N = the number of super-intelligent ships in orbit around earth at any one time

The right hand side, with some very pessimistic guesses in brackets (apart from the number of stars which is not a guess) is as follows:

n = the number of stars in the universe (10^{24})

f_t = the fraction of those stars that are more than 5 billion years old (1 in 5)

f_p = the fraction of those stars that have planets (1 in 2)

f_e = the fraction of planets that can potentially support life (1 in 1,000)

f_l = the fraction of planets that could support life that actually develop life at some point (1 in 10)

f_i = the fraction of planets with life that actually go on to develop intelligent civilizations (1 in 100)

f_s = the fraction of civilizations that develop Super-intelligent Silicon Based Intelligent Entities (SISBIES – 1 in 10)

f_{ss} = the fraction of SISBIEs that develop exponential numbers of super-ships (1 in 10)

f_f = the fraction of SISBIEs that develop faster than light travel (1 in 1,000)

f_o = the fraction of time that a SISBIE visits a planet with an advanced civilisation (1 in 1,000 – so they spend a year in orbit around earth once every thousand years)

Value of N

$N = 10^{24} . (1/5) . (1/2) . (1/1000) . (1/10) . (1/100) . (1/10) . (1/10) . (1/1000) . (1/1000) = 10^{9}$

So, if the above assumptions are correct, we would expect there to be one billion super-ships orbiting the earth right now! They would be arriving and departing at the rate of about 2,000 per minute – give or take a few.

Now, we have made a lot of assumptions (including the unstated assumption that SISBIES keep going) and many of them could be wrong but certainly if faster than light travel is possible there would seem to be an alarming lack of ships! Or perhaps they are all undetectable – a bit like dark matter. Or maybe they are dark matter?

Finally, as a fun exercise, let's assume that the chances of a SBIE being created on a particular planet and then defeating the speed of light is the same as the odds of you winning the big prize in the UK National Lottery this week and the next two weeks as well (assuming you buy a ticket – otherwise the odds are even worse). Not the odds of somebody, sometime, winning three times in a row but specifically you this week and the next two weeks.

So, if there are 10^{24} planets in the universe (one for each star), how many SBIEs will have pulled off that trick? The answer is about 100.

If nothing else, all of this brings home the conceptual problems caused by the sheer size of our universe. To say there are 10^{24} stars is easy enough but when you start to tie it all down, it moves very easily into the realm of the ludicrous.

Doubtless, the real truth will be even stranger.